ESL
English as a Second Language

Writing
Intermediate & Advanced

Mary Ellen Muñoz Page

Research & Education Association
Visit our website at
www.rea.com

Research & Education Association
258 Prospect Plains Road
Cranbury, New Jersey 08512
Email: info@rea.com

ESL Writing: Intermediate and Advanced

Published 2021

Printed in the United States of America

Library of Congress Control Number 2006931175

ISBN-13: 978-0-7386-0122-9
ISBN-10: 0-7386-0122-5

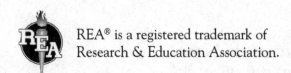

About REA

Founded in 1959, Research & Education Association (REA) is dedicated to publishing the finest and most effective educational materials—including study guides and test preps—for students of all ages.

Today, REA's wide-ranging catalog is a leading resource for students, teachers, and other professionals. Visit *www.rea.com* to see a complete listing of all our titles.

About This Book

Open a new world of opportunity by mastering the English language. *ESL Writing: Intermediate and Advanced* is truly for everyone, whether in school or on the job. This comprehensive guide serves as an ideal supplement to textbooks, language courses, and most other study aids and test preparation books. But with its thorough coverage of writing—including easy-to-follow grammar, discussion and writing exercises, glossary, and complete answer key—this book can be used by itself with confidence.

The ability to write and speak English effectively is necessary for success in *any* study area, whether it be English, science, mathematics, or social studies. Therefore, most standardized school and vocational tests—as well as the Test of English as a Foreign Language, or TOEFL—require that students demonstrate a command of the English language.

English writing and speaking skills are invaluable for getting a job and advancing in your chosen career. Employers (and their clients) often judge employees according to their ability to communicate effectively and in a productive way. This book—as well as REA's companion volume, *ESL Grammar: Intermediate and Advanced*—can help you take command of the English language and express yourself with precision…and success.

How to Use This Book

This book is one of the most straightforward study guides you will find. As you can see from the table of contents, all aspects of writing for ESL students are effectively covered. Each section contains clear explanations, simple examples, and ample exercises for you to practice and learn. The answer key at the back of the book is an ideal reference by which you can judge your progress, and the glossary stands ready to clear up any uncertainties about terms and their meanings.

REA wishes you all the best on your climb up the ladder to English-language mastery—and the success that you will enjoy in work and in life!

About the Author

Mary Ellen Muñoz Page is a former Bilingual Training Specialist and Spanish professor at the University of Florida in Gainesville. She received a B.A. in Spanish and history and an M.A. in Spanish, both from Case Western Reserve University, in Cleveland, Ohio. As a professor, Ms. Muñoz Page received three "Voyages of Discovery" mini-grants to develop cultural modules on Costa Rica, Guatemala, and Spain. Ms. Muñoz Page is also the author of books for the TOEFL Test (Test of English as a Foreign Language) and the Florida FTCE ESOL Examination K-12. She was selected for *Who's Who Among American Teachers* in 1996 and 1998.

Author Acknowledgments

This book is lovingly dedicated to my son, Louie Muñoz. To all my ESL students whose unceasing questions prompted the writing of this manual, I give my thanks. To Maureen Jennings, for her help in the final assembly of this book, my undying gratitude.

REA Acknowledgments

In addition to the author, we would like to thank Steven M. Gras, technical reviewer; Larry B. Kling, Editorial Director, for supervising development; Pam Weston, Publisher, for setting the quality standards for production integrity and managing the publication to completion; and Michael Reynolds, Editor, for project management.

Contents

Part I—Intermediate Writing

Part II—Advanced Writing

PART I
ESL
Intermediate Writing

Intermediate Writing

ESL

CHAPTER 1

Sentence Structure

Chapter 1
Sentence structure

OBJECTIVES FOR SENTENCE STRUCTURE

- Recognize essential components of a sentence
- Distinguish between fragments and complete sentences
- Rearrange words to form complete sentences and to convey complete ideas
- Realize that word groups containing subjects and verbs are not always complete sentences
- Recognize subordinate clauses and the conjunctions that introduce them
- Make all subjects and verbs agree
- Recognize prepositions and prepositional phrases
- Distinguish between clauses and phrases
- Distinguish between look-alike prepositional phrases (*behind/in back of*, *in/on*, etc.)
- Add words to phrases and clauses to create a complete thought
- Distinguish between sentences and phrases
- Recognize relative conjunctions and the words to which they refer
- Recognize gerunds and gerund phrases
- Identify the word that the gerund phrase modifies
- Recognize subordinate conjunctions and the clauses that they introduce
- Apply rules for punctuating phrases and clauses

FORMULAS

Subject + Verb + Complement

This story is interesting.
      S V   C

Bob lives in a large white house.
  S   V   C

We love to visit Grandma.
  S   V   C

Subject + Auxiliary + Negative + Verb + Complement

Tony did not see the movie.
  S aux neg V   C

The bells were not ringing at midnight.
    S   aux neg V   C

Norman could not read the fine print.
   S   aux neg V   C

Auxiliary + Subject + Verb + Complement?

Do you have any free time today?
Aux S V C   C

Have they posted the grades yet?
Aux   S V   C C

Would he support the candidate?

Aux   S   V   C

Aren't we supposed to visit your cousin next week?

Aux   NS   V   C   C

Auxiliary + Negative + Subject + Verb + Complement?

Isn't Peter going to the park with us?

Aux neg S   V   C   C

Shouldn't they speak louder?

Aux neg   S   V   C

Hasn't the teacher given the exam yet?

Aux neg   S   V   C

Question Word + Auxiliary + Subject + Verb + Direct Object + Complement

How many times did they call you last week?

QW   aux S   V D.O.   C

How long will you be collecting money for the charity?

QW   aux S   V   D.O.   C

When did Leslie invite us to the party?

QW aux   S   V   D.O.   C

Subject + Verb + Indirect Object (Pronoun) + Direct Object

Tom gave me the package.
　S　V　I.O.　　D.O.

Her father wrote her a long letter last week.
　　S　　V　I.O.　　D.O.　　C

The tour guide showed us the bell tower.
　　　S　　V　I.O.　　D.O.

Subject (Phrase) + Verb + Direct Object (Pronoun) + Indirect Object

Harry wrote them to me.
　S　　V　D.O.　I.O.

Mother read it to us.
　S　　V　D.O. I.O.

Dali painted it for Gala.
　S　　V　D.O. I.O.

Subject + Auxiliary + Negative + Verb + D.O. (Pronoun) + I.O. (Phrase)

The teacher is not giving them to her students.
　　S　aux neg　V　D.O.　　I.O.

Ted will not introduce us to his boss.
　S aux neg　　V　D.O.　I.O.

Mark had not written it to her.
　S　aux neg　V D.O. I.O.

Question Word + Auxiliary + Subject + Verb + I.O. (Pronoun) + D.O. (Phrase)

Why won't you give us the day off?
QW auxneg S V I.O.   D.O.

When are they bringing him his new car?
QW aux S   V   I.O.   D.O.

Where did Joe take you to eat dinner?
QW aux S V I.O.   D.O.

REVIEW OF WRITING COMPLETE SENTENCES

It is important to remember to use complete sentences when writing. There are four types of sentences: simple, compound, complex, and compound-complex.

Simple Sentences

Simple sentences contain subjects, verbs, and a complete thought in one independent clause. The subjects, verbs, and any objects may be single or compound.

Single subject + verb: The Seahawks won.
                        S   V

Simple subject, verb, and object: We saw that movie.
                                  S V   D.O.

Compound subject: Melvin and Harry live in Omaha.
                  S_1 S_2 V

Compound verb: <u>Gregory Hines acts and dances well.</u>

　　　　　　　S　　　　V$_1$　　　V$_2$

Compound object: <u>Shakespeare wrote plays and sonnets.</u>

　　　　　　　S　　　V　D.O.$_1$　　　D.O.$_2$

In the following sentences, there is a compound verb, but the whole sentence is not compound. The subject is the same, so it does not need to be repeated.

Tonight <u>I</u> <u>will read</u> a <u>book</u> or <u>watch</u> <u>television</u>.

　　　　S　　V$_1$　　D.O.$_1$　　V$_2$　　D.O.$_2$

<u>Sonia</u> <u>speaks</u> <u>English</u> but <u>does not write it</u>.

　　S　　V$_1$　　D.O.$_1$　　　V$_2$　　D.O.$_2$

Compound Sentences

In **compound sentences** two or more independent clauses are joined by a coordinating conjunction (**and, but, for, or, nor, yet, so**). There will be one subject and one verb in each clause, and each will convey a complete thought.

<u>Our class</u> <u>let out</u> early, **so** <u>we</u> <u>went</u> to the library.

　　S$_1$　　V$_1$　　　　　S$_1$　V$_2$

<u>Mary</u> <u>bought</u> <u>some ice cream</u>, **and** <u>we</u> <u>made</u> <u>chocolate sundaes</u>.

　　S$_1$　V$_1$　　　D.O.$_1$　　　　S$_2$　V$_2$　　　D.O.$_2$

Compound-complex sentences have at least two main clauses and one or two dependent clauses.

<u>Even though the weather is bad</u>, <u>Tracy is driving to North Carolina</u> and

　　　　　dependent clause　　　　　　　　　　　main clause

<u>Henry is flying to Phoenix</u>.

　　　main clause

Complex Sentences

Complex sentences contain one main clause and one or more dependent clauses.

While the children were getting dressed, their father prepared their breakfast.
               dependent clause   main clause

The students were late because there was an accident and the police set up a detour.
   main clause   dependent clause   dependent clause

Some dependent clauses can also begin with gerunds **[V + ing]**.

Flying through the air in a hot air balloon, the passengers enjoyed the ride.

Rising above the crowd, the balloon floated higher and higher.

The shortest sentence can contain only one word but still convey a complete idea. When we use the command form of the verb, the subject *you* is understood.

Go! Run! Write! Sing! Play!

In the following sentences, the verb is not a command; therefore, they are only simple sentences with compound verbs.

You write and speak English very well.

You act first and think later.

Incomplete Sentences, or Sentence Fragments

Unless the sentence is a command, there must be an expressed subject, a verb, and a complete thought. The following contain subjects and verbs, but they do not convey a complete idea.

When the lights went out   (What happened?)
           S   V

As <u>Julie</u> <u>drove</u> down the street   (What happened?)

    S   V

Note the problems with these and the method used to correct them.

INCOMPLETE: *Running for the bus at 8:00 in the morning.*

This is only a participial phrase. We don't know WHO was running or what happened.

COMPLETE: *Running for the bus at 8:00 in the morning, I slipped and fell.*

INCOMPLETE: *In the garden in front of the house.*

This example consists of two prepositional phrases, neither of which could ever be a subject; and there is no verb.

COMPLETE: *In the garden in front of the house is a beautiful gardenia bush.*

INCOMPLETE: *While the wind was blowing that afternoon.*

This is only an introductory phrase containing a subject (wind) and verb (was blowing), but it does not convey a complete thought. It does not tell what happened.

COMPLETE: *While the wind was blowing that day, our boat capsized.*

INCOMPLETE: *Climbed the tree as quickly as he could.*

This phrase has no subject. WHO climbed the tree?

COMPLETE: *The little boy climbed the tree as quickly as he could.*

INCOMPLETE: *Something big, hairy, and ugly standing by the window.*

This example contains no verb. Standing is only a gerund with no conjugated verb to indicate the tense.

COMPLETE: *Something big, hairy, and ugly WAS standing by the window.*

Nouns that are part of a prepositional phrase cannot be subjects.

EXERCISE 1

> Decide whether the following sentences are simple (S) or compound (C).

1. February usually has only twenty-eight days.   **(S)**

2. Nothing surprises me anymore.   **(S)**

3. We went to the movies and had some ice cream afterward.

4. Nick passed his medical exam, so he and his girlfriend went out to celebrate.

5. Roger and Germaine sing with a rock group.

6. I baked an apple pie, but I forgot to put cinnamon in it.

7. What the boss says and what she does are two different things.

8. Jaime wrote his uncle for some money, and his aunt sent him a check.

9. Everyone promised to attend, yet nobody showed up at the meeting.

10. The laws will change, or the people will rebel.

EXERCISE 2

> Read each of the following word groups and decide whether the word group is a complete sentence or a fragment. If it is a complete sentence, write the letter C in the margin; if it is a fragment, write F.

F 1. While young American girls are more independent in their lives for many reasons.

F 2. Their style, their horns, and the types of music they play.

___ 3. Having the independence of a good job and not having to depend on anyone financially.

___ 4. Exploring each thought to the fullest, Theo finally made the most important decision of his life.

___ 5. Athletic scholarships are not as easy to obtain as many people might think.

___ 6. Really looking forward to visiting Hawaii.

___ 7. Because Martha's never been there and has been waiting a long time to see it.

___ 8. Preparing the surface for painting, applying the paint, and cleaning your materials when the job is finished.

___ 9. Soccer and football are the most interesting games that people like to watch in winter.

___10. Whereas a construction worker uses wood, nails, a hammer, and cement.

EXERCISE 3

Read each of the following word groups and decide whether the word group is a complete sentence or a fragment. If it is a complete sentence, write the letter C in the margin; if it is a fragment, write F.

_C_ 1. The rapidity with which new knowledge has infiltrated the culture causes deep conflicts between the old and the new beliefs.

_C_ 2. The new government proposal caused a lot of money that would have gone into oil development to stay in the companies' treasuries.

___ 3. The second reason was more obvious than the first.

___ 4. Going to a party with your friends can be more fun than staying at home and doing nothing.

___ 5. Shoes, pair of shorts, socks, and three shirts were thrown around Rex's room.

___ 6. Or if he continues following you.

___ 7. In conclusion, about the American sports fans and how they view one another.

___ 8. For example, rock pits, the cutting down of small forests, coal mining that destroys the beauty of the countryside.

___ 9. Cruising on the water behind a boat with the wind and mist blowing in your face can be very exciting.

___10. Every business executive strives to be high enough on the corporate ladder so that his creativity will be recognized.

___11. To escape the arguments and discord between his parents or even that which exists between his parents and himself.

___12. Flowers brightening an otherwise gloomy stay in a hospital.

___13. Ever been to a sporting event?

___14. Even though there is a summer rainy season.

___15. First, you must consider the amount of room in a compact car before you decide to buy it.

___16. Having already accomplished an extremely difficult task that you normally could not do on your own.

___17. We enjoy attending a concert or reading a good adventure story.

___18. A football playing field is rectangular, whereas a baseball field is diamond shaped.

___19. In other words, protection from the cold, heat, and moisture.

___20. For instance, making the bed, cleaning the house, and washing the dishes.

WRITING EXERCISE

Write ten simple sentences about your family. Follow the examples.

My family is not very large. There are only five people. My parents are very intelligent.

WRITING EXERCISE

Write ten compound sentences about your classes.

Every day I walk to the university, and I arrive at 8:45. I talk with my friend in English class, but we must be quiet when the bell rings.

_____
_____
_____
_____
_____
_____

EMBEDDED QUESTIONS

embedded *Implanted*

Some noun clauses are introduced by question words: these are often referred to as embedded questions. The whole sentence in which they appear may or may not be a question. Because these question words now function as connectors, they introduce a dependent clause and do not convey a complete idea. When an embedded question appears in a declarative sentence, it differs from a regular question in that it does not ask for information. A period ends this type of sentence, not a question mark.

Normal question: How long will your friend be in the hospital?

The speaker expects a response from the listener—for example, two days, one week, a month.

Embedded question: I don't know how long she'll be there.

Notice that the word order is different for an embedded question. It follows this pattern:

> **subject + verb (phrase) + question word + subject + verb**

Normal question: When will they leave for Utah?

Embedded question: I'm not sure <u>when they will leave for Utah</u>.

Sometimes the embedded question is part of another question. In that case, the main-clause word order follows the regular pattern for questions, while the dependent clause follows the pattern for embedded questions. In these types of sentences, the speaker will expect a response from the listener, and a question mark ends the sentence. Because these question words now function as conjunctions, they introduce a dependent clause and do not convey a complete idea. The word order for this type of question follows a different pattern:

> **auxiliary + subject + verb + question word + subject + verb**

Normal question: How tall is Jennifer?

                           QW   V   S

Embedded question: Do you know how tall Jennifer is?

                           Aux S   V QW   S   V

— NOTE —

No auxiliary verb comes between the question word and the subject in an embedded question. When the auxiliary verb is omitted, there is a change in the main verb. The main verb will agree with the subject and show the tense.

Who <u>painted</u> the house?　　We do not know who <u>painted</u> the house.

Which dress <u>suits</u> you best?　　I'm not sure which dress <u>suits</u> me best.

EXERCISE 4

Underline the embedded questions in this conversation between two friends who have not seen each other for a few months and are catching up on some gossip.

Catching Up (colocar o papo em dia)

LISA: Hi, Della. I haven't seen you in a long time and have been wondering <u>what you have been doing lately</u>.

DELLA: Oh, I've been busy with my classes and my thesis. My adviser asked <u>what topic I had finally chosen</u>.

LISA: Have you decided what you are going to write?

DELLA: Not really. It's very difficult when you don't know what you want to do.

LISA: I hear that Fred's company is planning to transfer him, but he does not know where they are sending him.

DELLA: Yes, it's quite difficult for the family, because they do not know what they will do about getting a house. They are planning to sell their house here.

LISA: Have they decided yet how much they want for it?

DELLA: They need to talk with an appraiser first, and he will tell them how much it is worth.

LISA: I hear Julie got married some time ago.

DELLA: Yes, but I don't remember when she got married, and I don't know who the lucky guy is.

LISA: Oh, it's 3:00 and I have a 4:00 appointment. Call me tonight and let me know when we can get together.

DELLA: That's a great idea. I'll call after supper when it's quieter. See you later.

EXERCISE 5

Complete the following sentences, using the embedded question forms.

1. Whose books are these? I don't know *whose books these are*.

2. Where are they going tonight? I wish I knew *where they were going tonight*.

3. How many people will be attending the lecture? The program director isn't sure _____

4. Whom did David call? No one knows _____

5. Which of the dresses does Jane prefer? Can you tell me _____

6. Where does he come from? Let's ask him _____

7. How many cities did they visit on their vacation? Tom can't remember _____

8. How old are the twins? Can you guess _____?

9. What time did they leave for school? I don't remember _____

10. How does the microwave work? The demonstrator will explain _____

11. What happened to her car? No one is sure _____

12. What courses are his sisters studying? He doesn't know yet _____

13. What does "au revoir" mean in English? We can't remember _____

14. What did your mother buy at the supermarket? Please tell me _____

15. Which car is Jerry's? I wonder _____

16. When will the plane from New York arrive? Ask the ticket agent _____

17. Why did you miss class yesterday? Please explain _____

18. How many letters did she write to Beverly? I wonder _____

19. What was the lecture about? Can you tell me _____

20. How many stamps do I need for this package? Ask the postal clerk _____

TAG QUESTIONS

If someone makes a statement and is not sure it's true or wants to verify it, he can add a short question (a tag question) to it.

We're not having an exam
tomorrow, are we?

(The speaker's not sure about
the timing of the exam.)

There's a movie on television
tonight at 8:00, isn't there?

(The speaker asks for verification
about a program.)

Keep the following points in mind when using tag questions:

- The statement is always followed by a confirmation or tag in the form of a question.

    Sally won the prize, didn't she?

- If the statement is affirmative, then the tag is negative, and vice versa.

    The door is open, isn't it?   You're not wearing the jacket, are you?

- Statements containing *there* require a confirmation using *there*.

    There will be an election at the next meeting, won't there? Yes, there will.

- Statements containing *it* require a confirmation using *it*.

    It's going to rain, isn't it? Yes, it is.

- A contraction (*don't*, *wouldn't*, etc.) is usually used for negatives.

    You are studying statistics, aren't you?

    They do their homework every night, don't they?

- The subject of the statement and the question are the same, but the tag question requires the use of a pronoun.

    Harry's playing tennis, isn't he?

- The same auxiliary is used for both statement and question.

    Mary is going sailing with us, isn't she? You won't work late, will you?

    The group has gone to Cozumel, hasn't it?

- When no auxiliary accompanies a verb (past and present tenses), use forms of the verb **do** (do, does, did).

  > Salvador Dali painted (did paint) *The Persistence of Memory*, didn't he? (past)

  > Gloria Estefan sings (does sing) very well, doesn't she? (present)

- In American English, forms of the verb **have** may be used as the *main verb* or as *auxiliaries*. When they are used as the *main verb*, use **do**, **does**, **did** as the auxiliaries.

  > Beth has (does have) enough money for the dress, doesn't she?

  > We have (do have) the right tickets, don't we?

  > Calvin had (did have) a terrible cold last week, didn't he?

- When **has** or **have** is used as an **auxiliary**, repeat that form in the tag.

  > The Nelsons have visited you before, haven't they?

  > John has already seen that movie, hasn't he?

EXERCISE 6

Finish each of these sentences by using the correct tag question.

ex: Pete should study, ____(shouldn't he)____ ?

1. Jason is going to California next week, _____?

2. Mrs. Novak doesn't speak Korean, _doesn't she_____?

3. The children have their toys with them, _____?

4. That was such an easy assignment, _____?

5. The ladies are working late, _____?

6. There were many different flowers at the exhibit, _____?

7. The Masons took a trip to Europe last summer, _____?

8. You can play tennis well, _____?

9. He should practice his English more, _____?

10. They drink too much coffee, _____?

11. Mark answered the phone, _____?

12. The scouts will be going camping this weekend, _____?

13. The Chapmans moved to Arizona, _____?

14. The Yankees lost the last game, _____?

15. He wants to eat his steak right now, _____?

16. It snows a lot in the North, _____?

17. They have already seen that movie, _____?

18. You didn't find a new dress, _____?

19. Your friends live in the country, _____?

20. There will be a full moon out tonight, _____?

PHRASES

Phrases are groups of words that do not contain a subject or a verb, and do not express a complete idea. They may occur at the beginning, the middle, or the end of a complete sentence. You must add more words to a phrase in order to make it a complete sentence and give it complete meaning.

Prepositional Phrases

These begin with a preposition and are usually followed by *the* and a noun. These phrases indicate location, time, or manner or answer the questions *where,* *when,* or *how.* The following list of prepositions will help you identify prepositional phrases.

		preposition + the + noun a	
about	below	in front of	over
above	beside	in place of	past
according to	between	in regard to	since
across	beyond	in spite of	through
after	but (except)	in view of	to
ahead of	concerning	instead of	toward
along	contrary to	into	under
among	despite	like	underneath
apart from	down	near	until (till)
around	during	of	up
as	except	off	up to
as far as	for	on	upon
at	from	on account of	with
because of	in	out	within
before	in addition to	out of	without
behind	in back of	outside	

Look at the prepositional phrases in the following sentences.

Location (where):

Our friends parked the car in the driveway and came into the house.

Over the hill and through the woods we went to grandmother's house.

Time (when):

Our English class meets in the morning.

Your term paper must be finished before October 15.

Manner (how):

The thief escaped through the window.

Because she was not properly dressed, June felt out of place at the banquet.

EXERCISE 7

Underline the prepositional phrases in each of the following sentences. Some may contain more than one phrase.

1. After the movie we went to the soda shop for ice cream.

2. Here is a letter from your uncle.

3. You have until 4:30 to pay this bill.

4. The mother divided the cake among her children and their friends.

5. The movie star, in her elegant long dress, stood at the top of the spiral staircase.

6. Mario has been working in our office since 1985.

7. During spring recess, Ned and his friends went to the beach.

8. Nothing in this report seems to make any sense.

9. The English drink tea and have biscuits in the middle of the afternoon.

10. The boys were arguing about who would drive to the ball game.

11. The test did not seem too difficult for them.

12. Hal's office is located in front of the library.

13. Look behind the picture, and you will find the safe.

14. The airplane flew over the mountains.

15. Life forms at the bottom of the lake are very beautiful.

16. Mr. Jameson fell off the roof while he was installing his new antenna.

17. The police found the money between the refrigerator and the wall.

18. Sandra paid cash for the car.

19. Under the circumstances, I do not think that they are doing the right thing.

20. The Boy Scout helped the lady across the street.

EXERCISE 8

Read the following paragraph and underline the sixteen prepositional phrases.

Moving Day

Moving *into a new house* is a traumatic experience. If it is raining, the movers must try to keep the furniture *under plastic covers*. If they are not careful, they may drop some things out of the boxes and down the steps. When they finally get many things in the house, they just lay them in the corner so that the owners can put them in their proper places later. During the move, small objects get misplaced and the owners look under cartons, behind the furniture, and above the cupboards, hoping to find the missing items. For a number of days the owners look through their things, sort them, and put them away. Between one thing and another, they finally locate everything. After the move they can finally settle down and enjoy their new home.

WRITING EXERCISE

Write one sentence, using each of the prepositional phrases provided. Add words before or after to make complete sentences.

1. along the highway   *We drove along the highway to San Jose.*

2. except for Sue and Jim   *Except for Sue and Jim, everyone attended the party.*

3. in addition to photography _____

4. down the stairs _____

5. without your help _____

6. instead of driving to Phoenix _____

7. during December _____

8. above the refrigerator _____

9. throughout the 1970s _____

10. within the city limits _____

WRITING EXERCISE

Write a 75-word paragraph on one of the following topics, using at least eight prepositional phrases. Underline them. Be sure to reread your paragraph and correct any mistakes.

Life in a dormitory

Your arrival in America

Your moving experience

Getting to school on time

How you spend your weekends

EXERCISE 9

The following paragraph, "Arriving in America," is a Russian student's account of his family's journey to freedom. Prepositional phrases form the skeleton of the paragraph. Using the subjects, verbs, and complements from the chart below, fill in the required words to complete the meaning of each sentence. The letters in parentheses in the paragraph will tell you from which column to select the missing vocabulary. You may repeat the subjects, but use the verbs and complements only once. Look for key words and certain prepositions as clues for the verbs you will need.

Example: After many years of oppression, my family <u>decided to go</u> to America. We <u>stood</u> in line for many hours at the American Embassy to <u>get</u> a <u>passport</u>.

Subjects (S)	Verbs (V)	Complements (C)
We	Are	our papers
It	arrive	a passport
a man	ask	safely
He	cry	new customs
our family	decide to go	us
	fly	difficult
	get	English
	have to worry (negative)	very happy
	interview	
	learn	
	leave	
	live	
	look	
	prepare	
	sign	
	sit	
	stand	
	stay	
	study	
	was	

Arriving in America

After many years of oppression my family (V)_____ to America. We (V)_____ in line for many hours at the American Embassy to (V)_____ a (C) _____. In a special office a man (V)_____ us as he (V) _____ in a chair behind a big desk. He (V) _____ many questions about our family and our background. After almost three hours he (V) _____ our papers. We went home and (V) _____for a long journey. Our family (V) _____ without very much money and very few clothes. On the airplane to Italy (our first stop), we (V)_____ tears of joy. We (V)_____ in Italy for three months before our trip to Jacksonville, Florida. During this time we studied (C)_____. Finally, we (V) _____ for America. We (V) _____ for seven hours before the (S)_____ arrived (C) _____in the big city, our new home. Life was very (C) _____ for us at first. (S) _____ looked for jobs and learned new (C) _____. Today, we (V) _____ in our small apartment. We do not (V) _____ about problems. We are very (C) _____here in America.

Gerund Phrases

Gerunds are verb forms ending in *-ing*, and by themselves they function as nouns in a sentence. A gerund phrase begins with the [**V + ing**] form and is followed by a group of words. Gerund phrases do not convey a complete idea. This type of phrase usually comes at the beginning of a sentence, but it is also possible to find it at the end. Notice that when it comes at the beginning, there is a comma separating the gerund phrase and the main/independent clause (a sentence that can stand by itself). When the gerund phrase is at the beginning of the sentence, whatever follows the comma must be a person or an animal responsible for both actions. Look at the following examples:

Traveling through the Southwest, Sam learned a great deal about American culture.

Riding a bicycle and swimming daily, Ellen expects to lose weight.

In the first sentence, Sam traveled and Sam learned. In the second sentence, Ellen rides and swims, and Ellen expects.

When the subject does *not* perform both actions, the gerund phrase is just dangling, or hanging, in the sentence and not properly modifying the noun it is supposed to modify. For example:

Jumping out of the boat, the shark bit the man.   (The shark was not the one who jumped out of the boat; the man was.)

Hanging on one hinge, the carpenter replaced the broken door.   (The carpenter was not hanging on one hinge; the door was.)

In the following two sentences the modification problem does *not* exist:

We watched the pizza makers tossing the dough quickly and deftly.

Sandy won the prize, having written the best essay.

Another aspect to consider in using gerund phrases is that they can be preceded by the possessive form rather than the subject form.

INCORRECT: Mr. Bane objected to Mary taking the car yesterday.

CORRECT: Mr. Bane objected to Mary's taking the car yesterday.

Mr. Bane did not object to Mary, but rather to Mary's taking the car.

INCORRECT: I hope that Barbara accepting that position means an increase in salary.

CORRECT: I hope that Barbara's accepting that position means an increase in salary.

The speaker's wish refers to Barbara's accepting the position and not to Barbara herself.

EXERCISE 10

Underline the gerund phrases in each of the following sentences.

1. *Having already passed the street*, I turned around and went back.

2. The boss was pleased with his employees' finishing the project early.

3. While skiing in the mountains, we felt the cold wind hitting our cheeks.

4. Watching television non-stop for six hours, Ricky complained of eye problems.

5. Seeing the terrible accident, Cindy called the police.

6. Upon arriving at the pier, the captain of the boat dropped the anchor.

7. My cousin was afraid of my seeing her with my boyfriend.

8. Hovering over the airport, the airplane prepared to land.

9. I am worried about Hugh's water skiing without a life jacket.

10. Mona's taking so much medicine worries her doctor.

EXERCISE 11

Match the phrases in Column A with the clauses in Column B. The phrases may appear before or after the clause. Then rewrite the whole sentence, providing proper punctuation. (Hint: Commas are used when the clause that follows could be a complete sentence.)

Example: 1. Building an office complex in this area would create a problem for local residents.

Column A

1. building an office complex in this area

2. drinking and driving

3. swimming the English channel as quickly as she could,

4. hiding in the cellar,

5. shutting the window at night

6. flying through the air with the greatest of ease,

7. we listened to the wind

8. sitting uneasily in her boss's office,

9. wearing a ski cap in July,

10. hitting a ball near the end of the bat

11. falling from the tree,

12. cutting along the edge of the pattern

13. making peach pies

Column B

A. allows for a $\frac{5}{8}$" seam

B. blowing fiercely outside

C. Florence Chadwick broke the record

D. will provide more distance

E. would create a problem for local residents

F. Ryan looked ridiculous

G. don't mix

H. makes it quieter inside

I. the young girl escaped the soldier's search

J. the secretary waited for him to dictate the letters

K. the acrobats performed their stunts

L. made my grandmother very happy

M. Phil broke his arm in three places

EXERCISE 12

Match the phrases in Column A with the clauses in Column B. The phrases may appear before or after the clause. Then rewrite the whole sentence, providing proper punctuation. (Hint: Use a comma when the clause that follows could stand alone as a complete sentence.)

Example: 1. Cheryl's dropping the casserole sent pieces of glass flying everywhere.

Column A

1. Cheryl's dropping the casserole

2. repeatedly speaking in public

3. diving into the deep murky waters,

4. teaching younger children

5. washing the windows

6. sinking into the frigid water near the iceberg

7. leaving the house in a great hurry,

8. Seth's teacher was very much upset when she caught him

9. forgetting his lines in the play,

10. cooking eggs thoroughly

11. after providing more background light,

12. Jenny preferred to stay home at night

Column B

A. reading a good book or watching a movie

B. guards against food poisoning

C. provided a clearer and more beautiful view

D. writing in the new library book

E. sent pieces of glass flying everywhere

F. the photographer took a number of pictures

G. the actor decided to ad lib

H. the crew hoped to find the buried treasure

I. Tom forgot to lock the door

J. will make you feel more at ease

K. is quite a challenge

L. the great luxury liner disappeared

WRITING EXERCISE

Your teacher has just given you an assignment to write about your first experience registering at an American school. Think about the events surrounding this experience. As you list your ideas about what to write, use the gerund forms. Here are some of the ideas that Saud remembered from his first day on campus. Using the gerund phrases in the order that they are presented, fill in the blanks to provide the missing information.

signing up for classes   finding some of the sections already closed

running from office to office   hurrying to see my counselor

getting signatures   spending four hours on campus

filling out all of those forms   registering for classes

answering all the questions

When I came to the university, I did not think that 1. _____ would be so difficult. 2. _____ and 3. _____, I got lost many times. 4. _____ was something new to me. 5. _____ was difficult. 6. _____, I had to substitute other classes. 7. _____, I met an American who offered to help me. Finally, after 8. _____, I could go home. 9. _____ at this university was very frustrating!

EXERCISE 13

Here are the corrections one student made. After you read them, underline all of the gerund phrases.

Registering for Classes

When I came to this university, I did not think that *signing up for classes* would be so difficult. Running from office to office and getting signatures, I got lost many times. Filling out all of these forms was something new to me. Answering all the questions was difficult. Finding some of the sections already closed, I had to substitute other classes. Hurrying to see my counselor, I met an American who offered to help me. Finally, after spending four hours on campus, I could go home. Registering for classes at this university was very frustrating!

EXERCISE 14

In the following paragraph, one student started to describe his first trip to an American supermarket. Because he was in a hurry, he forgot to provide the main clause or verb for each sentence. Help him finish his assignment by adding subjects and verbs that will relate to the topic.

Shopping in an American Supermarket

Taking a shopping cart, I (1) *entered the store*. Walking up and down every aisle, (2) *I selected a number of items*. Looking at the prices, (3)_____. Asking the stock boy the location of several items, (4) _____. After surveying all the attractive vegetables, (5) _____. Then, after selecting two packages of meat, (6)_____. Holding my coupons and checkbook in my hand, (7)_____. Finally, putting the grocery bags in my car, (8)_____. Shopping in an American supermarket (9)_____.

SUBORDINATE CLAUSES

Subordinate, or dependent, clauses depend on the rest of the sentence to give them meaning. Although they may contain a subject and a verb, they do not convey a complete idea and, therefore, are not complete sentences.

Because it was raining is a clause that contains a subject and a verb, but it does not express a complete thought and leaves the reader wondering what happened. When you add a main clause, the idea becomes clear.

There were many accidents on the highway *because it was raining*.

Because it was raining, there were many accidents on the highway.

As long as Kim remains here is another dependent clause asking what will happen.

We feel safe *as long as Kim is here*.

As long as Kim is here, we feel safe.

Notice that there is a comma after the dependent clause when it comes first in the sentence. If the dependent clause comes in the middle of the sentence, there is no comma before it. If you look at both of the subordinate clauses, you will see that neither contains a complete thought. Imagine, for example, that you are conversing with someone when a third person enters the room, says either of the clauses, and walks out.

Would the clause *Because it was raining* give you a complete idea? No. Your next question would be "Well, what happened?"

Subordinate clauses can be used as **adverbs, adjectives,** or **nouns**.

Adverbial Clauses

These answer the questions *when*, *where*, *why* and *how*. Look at these examples of adverbial clauses.

While we were enjoying our picnic lunch, it began to rain.

When did it begin to rain? while we were enjoying our picnic lunch.

The little boy walked *as if his shoes were too tight.*

How did the little boy walk? as if his shoes were too tight.

The bank won't loan us the money because we don't have a job.

Why won't the bank loan us the money? because we don't have a job.

On a clear day in the mountains, there is beautiful scenery as far as the eye can see.

Where is the beautiful scenery? as far as the eye can see

The following conjunctions introduce adverbial clauses:

after	as though	so that	whichever
although	because	that	while
as	before	unless	whose
as far as	even though	until	why
as long as	if	when	
as if	provided that	whenever	
as soon as	since	where	

Adverbial clauses begin with any of the above-listed conjunctions except *when* and *where* (which introduce interrogatory statements).

You cannot take the course <u>unless</u> *you pay your tuition.*

<u>While</u> *Thomas had money in his pockets*, he was very happy.

Please tell me <u>where</u> *the meeting is.* I have forgotten.

In these examples, the clause is dependent on the rest of the sentence to give it meaning. However, if it appears at the beginning, it will be an independent, interrogatory clause.

When will your computer   We aren't sure <u>when</u> your computer
equipment arrive?   equipment will arrive.

Again, the clause beginning with **when** is dependent on the rest of the sentence. **When will your computer equipment arrive?** is an independent clause.

NOTE

After and *before* are *conjunctions* when a subject and verb follow them.

After I had written the letter, I mailed it.

Our friends invited us to their house *before we attended the football game.*

After and *before* function as *prepositions* and are part of a prepositional phrase when a noun or gerund follows them.

After the movie we stopped for ice cream.

Johnny brushed his teeth *before going to bed.*

WRITING EXERCISE

Using at least six different adverbial conjunctions from the list on the previous page, write ten sentences about your experiences in America. For example:

Even though my English is not perfect, I can communicate with many people.

Since I arrived in this city, I have had many different cultural experiences.

_____

_____

_____

_____

_____

_____

_____

_____

Adjective Clauses

Adjective clauses describe a noun and answer the questions *which* and *what + a noun.* The relative pronoun in each of the sentences below refers to the noun or pronoun before it, in the main clause. Because *who, whose,* and *which* are not used as question words here, the word groups that follow them are not complete sentences, only dependent clauses.

The following relative pronouns introduce adjective clauses:

that	which	who	whoever	whom	whomever	whose

The girl *who is wearing the green dress* is my cousin.
Which girl? the one who is wearing the green dress

The book that you bought yesterday is very rare.
Which book? the one that you bought yesterday.

Some of the places *which you have visited* are very interesting.
What places? the ones which you have visited

The gentleman *whom you met last night* is the president of the company.
Which gentleman? the one whom you met last night

Notice the difference between the following questions using **which, whose,** and **who** and those in the relative clauses. The examples below are complete sentences, while the others are dependent clauses.

> *Whose* sweater is that?
>
> *Which* of these bracelets do you prefer?
>
> *Which* shoe needs to be repaired?
>
> *Who* knows the right answer?

In formal speech always use **who** and **whom** for persons and **that** and **which** for things and animals.

Noun Clauses

Noun clauses answer the questions *who* and *what* or can be used as appositives, subjects, objects, or complements in the sentence.

> *That you should know the answer* surprises me. (subject)
> *What* surprises me? that you should know the answer
>
> Genghis Khan, *who ruled a very large empire*, was fierce and cruel.

This phrase set off by commas means the same as—or describes—Genghis Khan, the subject, and is, therefore, used as a noun (appositive).

> *Who* ruled a very large empire? Genghis Khan
> *Who* was fierce and cruel? Genghis Khan
>
> Sandy hopes *that she will get to visit China this summer.*
> *What* does Sandy hope? that she will get to visit China this summer. (direct object)

Look at the difference between the *who* clause under "Adjective Clauses" and this one. If you ask the *who* question for the first one, you will have to keep asking questions to get the complete answer.

> *Who* is wearing the green dress? the girl. *Which* girl? the one wearing the green dress.

EXERCISE 15

Underline the whole subordinate clause in each of the following sentences.

1. *Whenever you have time*, please call me.

2. I will buy *whichever sweater you like*.

3. Betty visited us before she moved away.

4. As you walked out the door, the phone rang.

5. I need to go shopping, since we do not have enough food for the party.

6. The gentleman who bought that house is the new dean of the law school.

7. If you get the information before Tuesday, please let me know.

8. Except for when he was ill, Peter has never missed a class.

9. As soon as you hear the results, send them to me.

10. Lynette looks as if she is enjoying the play.

11. Despite Bobby's constant criticism, he is a nice person.

12. Wherever you travel, take lots of pictures.

13. When the lights went out, we had to eat in the dark.

14. We had to wait a long time in the airport because the plane arrived late.

15. Even though the deadline had passed, the director agreed to accept our projects.

16. I haven't seen my nephew since he was seven years old.

17. Can you tell me where I can find the art museum?

18. The children whom you saw in the park live across the street.

19. That teacher, whose son is your student, plays the guitar rather well.

20. Nothing would happen to them if they took more precautions.

EXERCISE 16

Fill in the blanks with the correct conjunction from the list. Each may be used *only once*.

> despite   that   as far as   because   after
>
> when   until   even though   so that   whenever

Hurricane Warnings

(1) *Even though* scientists have advanced technology, they cannot control hurricanes. Late summer and early autumn are the worst times in the Tropics. (2)..... constant warnings, many people do not take the meteorologists' predictions seriously. (3)..... the latter issue bulletins, many run to the store to buy food for a party. They do not realize the danger (4)..... exists (5)..... it is on top of them. (6)..... they are concerned, the bad weather will not affect them. (7)..... the storm hits, however, they blame the authorities for not providing proper warnings. (8)..... the situation becomes life-threatening, these same people refuse to evacuate their homes and seek shelter. (9)..... of their reluctance to cooperate in an emergency, many problems arise, even death. All people living in these regions must take precautions (10)..... lives are not lost needlessly.

WRITING EXERCISE

Write a main clause containing a subject and a verb that when added before or after these subordinate clauses will form a complete sentence.

1. Unless you eat properly, *you will have many health problems*.

2. *The gentleman* whom you met this morning *is the new director*.

3. _____ why Shelly wants to study calculus.

4. Whenever you are in the neighborhood, _____

5. Although the weather is bad, _____

6. _____ so that you will know that I have arrived safely.

7. Since you already know about the party, _____

8. _____ where they are going.

9. After Tom has fixed the carburetor, _____

10. Except for the money in your pocket, _____

11. _____ even though I have tried hard to understand him.

12. _____ as if he had been awake all night.

13. Before you jump to conclusions, _____

14. As far as the committee knows, _____

EXERCISE 17

Select the conjunction that best completes the sentences in each section. Write the correct one in the space provided. Some forms may be repeated, and some sentences may have two possible answers.

| after | before | because | since | that |

1. _Before_ you answer any of the questions, please be sure that you read all the information.

2. _After_ he typed the paper, Bob placed it in the folder and gave it to the instructor.

3. _____ the computer broke down, our checks will be delayed until Monday.

4. _____ we did not follow the instructions, our request was denied.

5. _____ Melody should take over the secretary's duties was absurd.

6. _____ they began the archeological expedition, the scientists read the ancient Greek manuscripts.

7. _____ the snow had finally melted, the children were able to play outdoors.

8. _____ such a high-ranking official would betray his country is a mystery to us.

| if who whom as |

9. _____ the client looked through these samples, she selected the ones she wanted.

10. The counselor _____ you requested is busy right now, but he will be with you in about twenty minutes.

11. _____ we traveled farther north, we discovered that the weather got colder.

12. ____ you follow the rules in a foreign country, you should have no problem with the police.

13. The lecturer ____ is giving his presentation at 2:00 is an expert on the history of the Middle East.

14. It will affect the group ____ the director separates the members.

so that unless until while wherever

15. ____ you write more clearly, I will not be able to read this paper.

16. ____ you complete the program, you will not be placed in a job.

17. ____ you go, a small part of me will also go.

18. ____ the Aztec civilization was thriving, the Spanish conquistadors entered Mexico and began to replace it with their own culture.

19. ____ Rick buys a new car, he will have to take the bus to work.

20. We followed the road map ____ we would not get lost.

whichever although even though whose as if

21. ____ dress you make, you will be happy with it.

22. When I arrived in the room, Stan looked ____ he had seen a ghost.

23. ____ many students get good grades, they do not learn as much as they should.

24. ____ we worked late every evening and all weekend, we didn't finish the project by the deadline.

25. The applicant ____ resume you are reading is the most qualified for the job.

EXERCISE 18

Read the following essay and underline the ten subordinate clauses.

An Unusual Discovery

As Nazi Germany was invading France in 1940, an even more earth-shattering event was taking place. *While searching for a lost dog*, four French boys discovered quite by accident the prehistoric cave paintings of Lascaux. When the beam from their flashlight reflected against the lighter background on the walls of the cave, they could see some brightly colored animal paintings. These drawings were found not only on the wall, but also on many of the other surfaces that surrounded the astonished youths. All of the sketches that they saw depicted animals: deer, bison, and bulls.

After anthropologists had conducted considerable research, they learned that the cavemen used to paint pictures on the walls of their dwelling places just before they went hunting, hoping to bring home the animal they had painted. These drawings portrayed subjects in action. They were drawn to scale; however, some were considerably larger than those in real life.

Although the animal forms were perfectly proportioned, the human figures were far inferior by comparison. A well-known expert on prehistoric art verified that these paintings, which had been preserved for thousands of years in the airtight, moistureless caves, represented some of the greatest art treasures in all of France. Eight years later, after scientists had spent a great deal of time preserving the paintings, the public was finally able to see these historic marvels.

Despite the caveman's primitiveness, he had developed unique techniques for representing depth in his paintings and had found substances to create the colors needed to express his ideas. Thanks to a little lost dog, scientists have found one more link to man's past.

Vocabulary Expansion

earth-shattering – of great importance

Lascaux – site of Paleolithic cave paintings in southwestern France

cave – hollowed out area below the earth's surface

astonished – amazed, confounded

sketches – drawings

depicted – represented in picture or written form

bison – buffalo

dwelling places – where one lives

still-life – representation of an inanimate object in art

drawn to scale – portrayed in relation to proportion

marvels – things that evoke wonder, surprise

EXERCISE 19

Look at the subordinate clauses that you underlined in Exercise 18, and decide whether they are used as nouns, adjectives, or adverbs.

1.   6.

2.   7.

3.   8.

4.   9.

5.   10.

WRITING EXERCISE

Select one of the following topics and write a paragraph or two. Use at least six subordinate clauses and underline them. Use proper punctuation throughout.

1. A meeting with an old friend whom you have not seen in a few years or more

2. Problems facing international students in American colleges and universities

3. Your first attempt to play a sport or a game

4. Your first experience shopping in an American mall or a large department store

5. Your first airplane, train or boat ride

Intermediate Writing

ESL

CHAPTER 2

Introduction to Writing Paragraphs

Chapter 2
Introduction to writing paragraphs

INTRODUCTION TO WRITING

As you go through your daily routine, you realize that life is full of writing assignments. There are grocery lists, memos to yourself and others, a note or letter to a friend, a thank-you note, and reports for classes or for the boss. All of these contain varying degrees of formality, and you must write them appropriately for the intended purpose. Writing reflects the author's personality and gives others an immediate impression of his/her talents, neatness, sophistication, and potential. Job interviewers form immediate opinions of applicants based on applications they submit. Writing tells a great deal about an individual. When you write, keep the following points in mind:

- Never begin to write until you fully understand the assignment.

- Ask questions when you are in doubt.

- Keep looking back at the title and the thesis statement to be sure that you are sticking to the topic.

- Always select a topic that is familiar to you when you have a choice. Ideas will flow more freely, and it will take less time to write.

- Make your readers feel emotionally involved by your choice of words.

- Narrow the topic if it is too broad.

- Spend time brainstorming to get enough ideas to complete the assignment.

- Write down all the ideas that come to mind.

- Organize and regroup these ideas.

- Limit the total number of ideas that you plan to develop.

- Make an outline, even a sketchy one, so that you have a plan from which your ideas will flow smoothly.

- Start with generalities and follow with supporting details.

- Choose words carefully. Incorrect word usage can lead to misunderstanding, embarrassment, or a bad impression.

- Always keep a dictionary beside your desk to check on spelling, meaning, word division into syllables, parts of speech, and idiomatic expressions.

- Use *Roget's Thesaurus* to find synonyms and antonyms to expand your vocabulary and to avoid constant repetition of the same words.

- Avoid clichés, overworked expressions that writers use when they can't come up with something original.

OBJECTIVES FOR WRITING

- Learn to select topics wisely

- Learn to narrow or expand on topics

- Learn to focus on only one aspect of the topic

- Learn to brainstorm, regroup, and eliminate

- Recognize the three principal parts of an essay

- Write good thesis statements and conclusions

- Distinguish between thesis statements and topic sentences

- Learn to write good supporting details to develop each topic sentence

- Learn how to write good conclusions

- Learn the proper outlining format

- Concentrate on the appropriate vocabulary for the audience who will read your compositions

- Distinguish between slang and formal English

- Eliminate verbosity

SLANG VS. FORMAL ENGLISH

Use slang only to enhance the mood you are trying to create.

JARGON

SLANG	FORMAL
kid	child
bunch of	group of
out of it	incoherent
chopper	helicopter
chow	food
get mugged	be attacked from behind
wino	person addicted to wine
moocher	person who begs shamelessly
cool cat	person (usually male) thought by his peers to display good taste in dress and manners
zits	facial pimples, acne
chick	nice-looking young woman
hoofer	professional dancer
boob tube, idiot box	television
boom box	large, noisy, portable radio
quack	person who pretends to be a doctor

Slang – gíria

hoopla	excitement
horse around	get into mischief
whoop it up	have a good time

Profane language and street talk do not enhance formal writing. They detract from it and often upset readers to the extent that they may lose interest in what you are saying.

VERBOSITY

Verbosity, the use of many words when one or two will do, often occurs when a writer really has nothing to say. The expression "in a joyful mood" for example, could best be said in one word: *joyfully*. Without a lot of excess words, writers' ideas will be more clearly expressed, and readers will have no problem understanding them.

Have you ever asked someone how he or she felt and then found yourself listening to half an hour of silly minor problems? In a way, verbosity is like this. Many students become verbose because they fail to brainstorm sufficiently for their writing assignments. If they have a 300- to 500-word assignment and do not think of enough supporting details for their paper, they add a lot of extra words just to fill up space. Verbosity can result when phrases are used to modify verbs when writers should be using adverbs.

Boris acted *in a thoughtful manner*.

Boris acted thoughtfully.

The rescue workers freed the victims *in a quick manner and with ease*.

The rescue workers freed the victims quickly and easily.

By avoiding verbosity, writers can come to the point and not lose an audience who must read through excessive vocabulary just to find out what is going on.

Also related to verbosity is *redundancy*, which occurs when words having the same meaning are placed together. In describing an object, some writers might be tempted to use the following.

INCORRECT: The bookcase was heavier in weight, darker in color, and more expensive in price than the one for which Gina was looking. (22 words)

CORRECT: The bookcase was heavier, darker, and more expensive than what Gina wanted. (12 words)

INCORRECT: The place where you should buy your clothes is the Dress Alive. (12 words)

CORRECT: You should shop at Dress Alive. (6 words)

Avoid the following redundant expressions.

Redundant	Correct
surrounded on all sides	surrounded by
the reason is because	because
coerce by force	coerce; force
new innovations	innovations; new ideas
repeat again	repeat
two twins	twins
join together	join
the time when	when
advance forward	advance; move forward
return back	return
these two both	both; the two
sufficient enough	sufficient; enough

and . . . also	and; also
at the place where	where; at
retreat back	retreat; go back
someone he	someone; he
people they	people; they
separate apart	separate
each and every	each; every
more + [adjective + ER]	adjective + ER
most + [adjective + EST]	adjective + EST
many kinds of	many
truly and really	certainly; truly
in the whole wide world	in the world
the reason why	the reason
because of the fact that	because
savage and wild	wild; savage

Can you think of any other redundant expressions that you hear others use?

EXERCISE 20

Read the following story and, using the list provided on the previous page, eliminate the underlined verbose and redundant expressions. Then rewrite the revised paragraph.

Friday the Thirteenth

It was Friday and I was looking forward to the weekend <u>the time when</u> I could relax. Despite some gray clouds in the sky, I left my umbrella and raincoat at home. Because of a sudden thunderstorm, there was a bad accident on the road, and <u>that was the reason why</u> I arrived late for work. Consequently, <u>my boss he</u> was very angry and disappointed because I was not <u>at the place where the meeting was</u> to give my report at 8:30. When I put my report in the copy machine, nothing happened, so <u>I repeated the process again</u>, and as a result of a malfunction, it shredded my report instead of printing it. Since the only other copy was at home, I told my boss that I would <u>return back home</u> to get it and have it on his desk in <u>sufficient enough</u> time to submit it to the committee. I had no umbrella and consequently got wet <u>advancing forward</u> as fast as I could to the parking lot <u>to the place where</u> I had parked my car. I decided to change clothes when I <u>returned back home</u>. Then as I was hurrying, I bumped the corner of the coffee table and got a run in my stockings. Because my report arrived late, the committee postponed its decision on the project. So another Friday the thirteenth had passed, and I became one of its victims of bad luck. I decided to <u>retreat back home</u> and try to forget everything that happened <u>and also</u> the shredded report.

EXERCISE 21

Correct all verbosity and redundancy errors. Then rewrite the paragraph.

African Flora and Fauna

The continent of Africa has the <u>most richest</u> variety of flora and fauna in the <u>whole wide world</u>. <u>Because of the fact that</u> it is located in tropical jungle areas, there are <u>many kinds of</u> lush plants. These plants that <u>surround</u> the oases of the deserts <u>on all sides</u> are very beautiful. This continent can claim the diversity of animal fauna that breeds and roams the jungle areas. <u>Many kinds of</u> species of birds and snakes fly and slither throughout the area. Camels, lions, giraffes, elephants, gazelles, tigers, zebras, and antelopes <u>they</u> are just a few of the <u>savage and wild</u> animals that roam the grassy savannas <u>each and every</u> day. Besides the savannas, its physical geographic features include tropical rain forests, the Atlas Mountains, and the hot and arid Sahara, Kalahari, and Namib deserts. All of these natural phenomena—the savannas, the tropical rain forests, the mountains, and the deserts—provide shelter for a variety of <u>different kinds of</u> animal species. <u>Truly and really for certain</u>, the continent of Africa provides the <u>most greatest</u> diversity of <u>plant vegetation, flora, animals, and fauna</u> in the <u>whole wide world</u>.

VOCABULARY EXPANSION

flora – flowers and other vegetation of a region

fauna – variety of animals of a particular region

jungle – large area filled with dense vegetation and wild animals

oases – (plural of oasis) green area in the middle of a desert

breeds – (v.) reproduces

slither – move like a snake

savage – wild

savannas – large tropical grassland with few trees

camel – large domesticated mammal with a humped back and long neck

gazelle – a small swift antelope with large eyes

antelope – a swift, horned animal resembling a deer

OBJECTIVES FOR WRITING PARAGRAPHS

- Use proper transition words to move smoothly from one idea to another

- Avoid short, choppy sentences

- Use appropriate conjunctions and transitions to combine short, choppy sentences into smoothly flowing ones

- Create compound-complex sentences

- Write smooth-flowing paragraphs

- Eliminate excess words

- Distinguish among interchangeable transitions and those that are similar in meaning but have different grammatical structures

- Learn what constitutes a paragraph and how it differs from an essay

- Distinguish among the different types of paragraphs: introductory, developmental, and conclusion

WHAT IS A PARAGRAPH?

A paragraph is a group of sentences dealing with one topic or idea. It begins with a topic sentence to which all the supporting sentences that follow directly relate. The topic sentence or thesis statement indicates the main idea and the method the writer will use to develop the paragraph. The stronger the support presented in the paragraph for the thesis statement, the better the paragraph. The final sentence should serve as a conclusion. There is no specific length for a paragraph.

Multi-paragraph works, called essays, examine several aspects of a topic, instead of just one. They begin with an introductory paragraph, which presents the theme of the essay and the method of approach to be used to develop the topic. The body paragraphs follow, providing supporting details and transitioning the reader from the start to the conclusion of the essay. The conclusion ends the essay and ties the whole paper together, showing that the essay has accomplished what it set out to do.

In a paragraph the ideas can proceed from a general statement to more specific ones. This type is called a *deductive reasoning* paragraph. Using this paragraph form, writers can start with the least important details and move to the most important ones. This method keeps the audience reading until the very end. It is also most effective in proving a point in a persuasion paper.

Thesis statement: The government needs to establish a 55 mph speed limit on all major highways.

Detail: At lower speeds cars consume less gasoline.

Detail: Drivers maintain greater control of their vehicles.

Detail: Lower pollution levels create a cleaner atmosphere and save the ozone layer.

Another type of paragraph is the *inductive reasoning* paragraph. Here, writers start with a specific statement and move to the general. This method is most effective when you want your readers to reach their own conclusions.

Detail: Review your class notes as soon as possible after writing them.

Detail: Study with a small group of dedicated classmates.

Detail: Create easy-to-learn note cards.

Thesis statement: Following a dedicated study pattern will help you do well on tests.

It is also possible to start a paragraph with a dilemma, and then offer a type of solution in the sentence that follows. The rest of the paragraph will consist of a number of sentences that support the proposed solution. The more you write, the easier it will be to decide on the appropriate method for whatever you are writing.

Now you will begin your detailed study of writing paragraphs and then make the transition to combining various paragraphs into an essay. For now, you will write a short paragraph that begins with a topic sentence that will get your readers' attention and let them know what you plan to tell them. Then you will come up with at least seven sentences that will present details to support or develop your paragraph. Finally, you will write a conclusion that tells your readers that this is the end of your writing and that you have nothing more to say.

The following paragraph, "The Little Big Horn," serves as a model. Look at these conventions you should follow:

• Center the title. Do not underline it.

• Capitalize the most important words of the title, always the first word, and all the proper nouns.

- Other proper nouns to be capitalized throughout the paragraph are General (a title followed by a name) George Armstrong Custer, Sioux Indians, Montana, Americans, Rosebud Ridge, Wolf Mountain.

- Use a capital letter for the first word of every sentence.

- Indent the first line of every paragraph if you are writing a longer paper.

- Use appropriate punctuation throughout.

- Write a good thesis statement (usually one sentence for a paragraph composition or the first paragraph of longer papers) or a topic sentence at the beginning of each paragraph (for essays).

- Be sure that all information that follows relates to the thesis statement.

- In the paragraph below, everything must relate to and support the statement "The Battle of the Little Big Horn was a great American tragedy."

- Provide good supporting details.

- Write a short conclusion that lets your readers know that you have nothing more to say. In this paragraph you would write "The cost for peace was very high, as many Americans lost their lives that hot summer day in Montana."

Now read the paragraph and look for the details and elements mentioned above.

The Little Big Horn

The Battle of the Little Big Horn was a great American tragedy. On June 26, 1876, General George Armstrong Custer and his soldiers were trespassing on Sioux Indian land in Montana, searching for gold. They wanted to find out how many Indians were living in a nearby village. At first they saw only a few on that quiet summer day. Suddenly, thousands circled the Rosebud Ridge and Wolf Mountain area. The Indians surrounded the 250 American soldiers, who saw no immediate reinforcements approaching. The brave soldiers fought off the Indians for three hours, but the Indians' superior numbers overwhelmed them. The Indians massacred all of them. History recalls the battle more for the mystery surrounding it than for the loss of 250 American lives. The Indians wanted to live in peace on their land, but white men searching for gold refused to leave them alone. The cost for peace was very high, as many Americans lost their lives that hot summer day in Montana. Today a simple monument commemorates this tragic event in America.

SELECTING A TOPIC

Possibly the most difficult phase of writing is that of selecting a topic. If you have to write weekly journals, you will probably find that you wait until the last minute to write them because you just cannot think of anything to say. If your instructor does not provide you with any ideas, the task becomes even more difficult. When you have a choice, however, you might want to keep these points in mind:

• Never select a topic unfamiliar to you.

• Find a subject that you have discussed in conversation or about which you have read a lot.

• Focus on a particular aspect of the topic, or your writing will be too long for the time allotted.

• Do not write on a subject that is very limited.

• Brainstorm your topic a little before you make the final decision. If you cannot come up with many ideas during the brainstorming, then it will be difficult to add more during the actual writing.

• Write on something about which you feel deeply, either positively or negatively.

Keep a notebook in which you can jot down your thoughts during the day: an idea that comes to you, a conversation you have had, something exciting or interesting that you have seen, or any observation you might have made. You may come up with ten ideas in one day, and after a few months, those might be enough to fill ten journals. Be observant. Look at what you see around you. Pay attention to what others say and do. Finding the right topic is not difficult if you know where to look.

On some exams, there will be only one topic, and you must write only on the one chosen for you. If you write on another topic, you will receive no credit for your work. In classes other than English, you will also have essays to write on specific topics not of your own choosing. If you have little to say on the one selected for you, write whatever you can and develop it as best you can.

If you have no brothers or sisters and you need to write about sibling rivalry, think of your friends and others you know who have siblings. What sorts of problems do you see in their relationships? Write about these. If you need to write about a sporting event, but you have never attended one, think about comments that others have made and write about them. If you play a sport, work around that idea. If you are to write about the topic "Brushing Your Teeth," and assuming that you are not in the dental profession, you could develop a process paragraph. However, if you are a professional in this field, you could write a lengthier paper based on your background and technical knowledge of the subject. All in all, it will take you longer to brainstorm an unfamiliar topic than one that you have experienced. *Do not write on a completely unrelated topic.*

If your topic seems too broad, focus on one particular aspect; otherwise, you will be writing a very long composition. If you are not limited to a method, you can write a narrative, description, comparison, or contrast paper.

Whether your instructor gives you a topic or you select one from a number of possibilities, look at it and decide whether it is *just right*, *too broad*, or *too narrow*. One that is too broad forces you to write a great deal and will not provide a focus. You will not come up with many details. Topics that are too narrow limit you. After writing a few sentences, you will find that you have nothing more to say and you will not be able to provide enough details to support your thesis. You must also keep in mind the required length of your paper. If you have a ten-page term paper to write, your scope will be somewhat wider than if you attempt to discuss the same topic in a three-paragraph essay.

EXERCISE 22

Look at the following topics and decide whether they are just right, too narrow, or too broad for you to write a three to five paragraph essay on. Remember that a topic that is too narrow cannot be developed in three to five paragraphs. You will probably write one or two paragraphs and find that you have nothing more to say about your topic. On the other hand, one that is too broad will take many more paragraphs to develop because you will have too much to say for a short essay. Use the following letters to indicate the type:

OK = just right   **B = too broad**   **N = too narrow**

_____ 1. A memorable birthday

_____ 2. Albert Einstein

_____ 3. Alcohol and drug abuse

_____ 4. Animals in the zoo

_____ 5. Backgammon

_____ 6. Big cities

_____ 7. Boyfriends

_____ 8. Building your own home

_____ 9. Cleaning the bathtub

_____10. Computer operators

_____11. Dates

_____12. Dogs

_____13. Dress codes

_____14. Eating with chopsticks

_____15. Fear of snakes

_____16. Fears

_____17. Football and baseball

_____18. Hang gliding

_____19. Hanging a framed picture

_____20. Indian folklore

_____21. Labor unions

_____22. Last summer's vacation

_____23. Learning to tie your shoelaces

_____24. Microscopic insects

_____25. Money problems

_____26. Mountain climbing in Europe

_____27. My most boring date

_____28. Niagara Falls

_____29. Pets

_____30. Physical fitness

_____31. Preparing lasagna

_____32. Preparing toast for breakfast

_____33. Riding a horse

_____34. Saving time and money at the supermarket

_____35. Signing an autograph

_____36. Sports

_____37. Spring break in Fort Lauderdale, Florida

_____38. Summer activities

_____39. Swimmers

_____40. The "preppie" look

CONSIDERING YOUR AUDIENCE

public

It is very important to consider the audience in your writing. You need to adjust your tone, vocabulary, and whole presentation to a specific group. If you are writing about a process, and your audience is a group of fifth graders, you do not want to use highly technical vocabulary or explain a complicated procedure to them. You would not, for example, select your topic on an advanced science project for a group of younger students.

Today on television, viewers can see some very sophisticated cartoons with subtle meanings that children miss. Either the writers aim at the wrong audience or really do not care whether the children understand or not. Also consider in your own lives how you select certain words in dealing with different people. You would not, for example, use some of the same vocabulary (possibly slang) in dealing with your instructors as you might use with your friends at lunch time.

Look at the following topics and decide who the audience might be.

TOPIC	**AUDIENCE**
Preparation of your favorite food	*friends, fellow students*
A trip to the zoo (real or imaginary)	*children*
The death penalty	_____
Drugs on your campus	_____
Your college's admissions policy	_____
Athletic scholarships	_____
Cheating on exams	_____
Studying required courses	_____
Working the night shift	_____
Need for physical fitness	_____
Women's rights	_____
Dating	_____
Marriage counseling	_____
Computer dating	_____

BRAINSTORMING

Brainstorming is the second stage of the writing process and consists of listing everything that comes to mind on a particular topic. Depending on the length of the essay, this process could take from five minutes to a number of days or weeks. In the case of the former, if you have an in-class timed writing, you should allow yourself about five minutes to list every idea on your topic. If you come up with a short list, then you had better find another topic quickly. If you have a long list, you can always regroup and focus on one particular aspect of the topic.

For a simple one-paragraph writing, you don't need a great deal of information, but you do need a number of key words to provide at least *three supporting details*.

The Spanish call this concept *una lluvia de ideas*, a shower of ideas. This a good image because you can imagine all the ideas dropping from the sky.

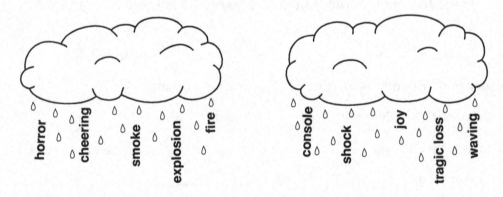

Read the following paragraph about the tragic *Challenger* liftoff at Cape Canaveral and notice how the writer uses adjectives and other details to make the paragraph come alive.

BRAINSTORMING

tragic loss	crowd	cheering	smiling	waving
unexpected cloud	smoke	fire	explosion	
emotional changes	joy to shock	horror	family console one another	

> ## The Challenger Tragedy
>
> *The U.S. Space Program has suffered many losses, but the most tragic occurred in January 1986.* As the spaceship *Challenger* departed the launchpad, the crowd stood cheering, smiling, and waving their arms wildly. Suddenly, an unexpected cloud of smoke, then fire, and finally an explosion thirteen miles up changed the joy to shock, horror, and numbness. Though unbelieving at first, the family members clutched at their loved ones, trying to console one another in the face of this terrible loss. Challenger *and its seven crew members would go down in history as NASA's most tragic loss.*

If your topic is *cars*, but you do not own one, focus on describing a particular car that you have seen or liked. Think about the ones your friends have and discuss what you feel are the joys, problems, advantages, or repairs that cars entail. It is possible to write a good paragraph even if you are not as familiar with the topic as you wish to be. Do not waste time writing until you have brainstormed enough to know whether you have enough information to develop the topic.

BRAINSTORMING

A Car for Andy

work	school
errands for mother	long distance for all jobs
waiter, usher	collects aluminum cans and newspapers
saves money	

If you were to write a complete sentence outline for a paragraph titled "A Car for Andy," this is what it would look like. Keep in mind, however, that this is a very long outline for such a short writing.

Outline

- Andy needs a car.
- He works part-time.
- He goes to school.

- He lives far from work and school.

- He runs errands for his mother.

- Andy plans to earn the money.

- He has a job as a waiter.

- He works at the movie theater.

- He collects aluminum cans and newspapers to recycle.

A topic outline is usually shorter, providing all the same information but in a more concise format. You would still have to follow the rules for parallelism. If you started each line by using an adjective, for example, you would have to continue in the same format throughout the outline. Using "A Car for Andy" as the topic, you can create the following outline. You still need to use complete sentences for your thesis statement and conclusion.

A Car for Andy

Need for car
    Part-time work
    School
    Long distance
    Errands for mother
Jobs
    Waiter
    Usher
    Aluminum and paper collector

Which of the following is the best first sentence (thesis statement) for this paragraph? Does it relate to *all* of the ideas in the outline?

- Andy is earning money to buy a car.

- Andy is working hard to get a car.

- Andy is a hardworking young man who needs better transportation to get back and forth from school to his job.

The last is the best because it includes everything from the outline. Now look at the paragraph below, which was written using the outline.

A Car for Andy

Andy is a hardworking young man who needs better transportation to get back and forth from school to his jobs. He studies at the university every day from 8 until 12. At noon he heads for the Paradise Inn, where he works as a waiter from 12:30 to 5:00, five days per week. Since the restaurant is near the university, he can ride his bicycle to work. After work he hurries home to run errands for his mother. If Andy had a car, he could save a lot of time and running around. Four weeks ago he decided to buy a car as soon as he got enough money. On weekends he works as an usher at the local movie theater. He also collects aluminum cans and newspapers so that he can save enough money for his car. If Andy keeps on working and saving money, he will have his car in a few months, and he will be able to get to work and run his errands without any problems.

BRAINSTORMING

Pets

do not have any

think about an imaginary one

a small stuffed or plastic one you had as a child

their care and feeding

problems

dependent/independent

self-grooming

a story you read or a movie you saw about an animal

the comfort they provide for the sick or for older people

a visit to someone's house where there was a pet

grooming

health care

food

play area

affectionate/indifferent

large/small

requires grooming

training

Dennis moved into a large apartment and decided to purchase a pet to keep himself company. *Before he went looking for an animal, he realized he had to decide what kind to get.* Since cats and dogs were his favorite, he narrowed his choice to two. *Dennis decided to contrast them to see which would be the better animal to have around the house.* **Detail:** While dogs are usually dependent on their masters, cats tend to be rather independent. **Detail:** The breed of dog determines its size, yet cats, no matter the breed, are small. **Detail:** Cats are very clean pets. **Detail:** They use a litter box and consistently lick themselves to keep clean. **Detail:** However, owners must groom and bathe dogs to keep them from smelling. **Detail:** The only training cats learn is how to use a litter box. **Detail:** On the other hand, dogs can learn to fetch, heel, and sit and do various other tricks. **Detail:** Even though cats are not as affectionate as dogs, both animals provide companionship to their masters. After evaluating numerous characteristics between cats and dogs, Dennis finally made a decision. **Conclusion:** *Although a cat would not hinder his fast paced life-style, a dog would protect him and provide him with the affection and companionship he valued the most.* Dennis could not wait to get to the pet shop to select his new companion.

BRAINSTORMING

Being a Mother

combination of mother, teacher, nurse, chauffeur, typist	loving
cook, seamstress	creative
always on call	peacemaker
low-paying job	patient
compassionate	unselfish

Which of the following would be the best introduction statement?

Being a mother is a combination of many things.

Mothers have many jobs.

Being a mother is one of the most difficult but rewarding jobs in the world.

The third is the best because it includes *all* of the information of the brainstorming. The adjectives *difficult* and *rewarding* indicate what the writer will be emphasizing.

Being a Mother

Being a mother is one of the most difficult but rewarding jobs in the world. A mother serves many roles: teacher, nurse, chauffeur, typist, cook, seamstress, and friend. Possibly none is more important than her role as a teacher. She serves as a role model for her children. They pick up on everything she does and repeat her actions. As a nurse, she is always available to clean a wound, put a bandage on it, and kiss it to make it better. She offers compassion and wipes away the tears.

Her special soup and medicine will cure just about any pain. She sacrifices an afternoon out to nurse her children back to health. A mother is always around to drive her children to sports events, to the dentist or to the doctor, to the dance lesson, or to shop for new clothes. She is there to make her children's favorite foods, their special cakes, particularly for their birthdays. Her photographs of these wonderful events grace many albums. Even though she is strict at times, she still loves her children dearly and wants the best for them. *Mothers have the most important and most demanding job in the world.*

VOCABULARY EXPANSION

chauffeur – one who drives a car

seamstress – woman who sews

emulate – (v.) to imitate

compassion – sympathy

strict – demanding discipline

Imagine that your topic is "Roommates." At first glance you see that this is a very broad subject and that you will have to focus on only one aspect of it. You then decide to write about your own roommate, so you begin to brainstorm, and after five minutes, you come up with the following list of facts.

lazy

hates housework

smokes too much

needs whole table to work on his projects

throws dirty clothes under the bed

doesn't empty the ashtrays

throws empty pop cans on the floor

works out in the gym every afternoon

generous with time and money

plays hard rock music on the stereo

cooks well but never cleans up

has a nice girlfriend

throws wet towels on the bathroom floor after showering

likes fashionable clothes

talks a lot on the telephone

never makes his bed

belongs to a fraternity

sings in the shower

dances well

gets good grades

has lots of friends

CLUSTERING

Clustering, or the regrouping of all similar elements, will help you organize your ideas so that you will have enough, but not too many, for the essay you are going to write. If there are too many details to incorporate into your essay within the given time, you need to regroup and/or eliminate some, focusing on only one aspect of the topic. All the characteristics of the roommate fit into three categories. This is how you would cluster them.

annoying	admirable	general
hates housework	has nice girlfriend	lazy
smokes too much	cooks well	works out in the gym every day
doesn't empty ashtrays	likes fashionable clothes	sings in the shower
throws empty cans on floor	belongs to a fraternity	
plays hard rock on stereo	dances well	
never makes bed	gets good grades	
uses whole table for projects	has lots of friends	
talks on phone a lot		

Look at the clustering graphic on the following page.

The largest grouping of ideas occurs in the first category in the table on the previous page headed *annoying,* so you should choose this category to write about. You can subdivide it further into two other categories: slovenliness and laziness. You will need to develop one of these characteristics in each of the paragraphs that form the body of your essay. Provide as many supporting details as you can for each of the key words. Look at the following word family:

slob (n) – an untidy or messy person; not neat

sloppy (adj) – untidy or messy

slovenliness (n) – lack of being neat

The World's Sloppiest Roommate

When students have to live in a dormitory, they cannot always choose the person with whom they will share their lives for the next semester or even year. If both have entirely different lifestyles, many problems can result. My roommate's habits are radically different from mine. *He has two most annoying qualities, which are slovenliness and laziness.*

Brett likes fashionable clothes and dresses very "preppie," but *around the dorm he is a perfect slob.* After working out in the gym every afternoon, he showers and leaves a mess in the bathroom. The other day I went in to comb my hair and found two dripping-wet towels thrown in the corner. He left dirty soap scum in the tub and dropped shampoo all over the bath mat. After his shower he smokes a cigarette and drinks a cold beer, but somehow can't find his way to the wastebasket to discard his trash. Last week I counted 25 butts in the ashtray and 10 empty cans next to the sofa.

As if this weren't enough, *he is so lazy that his friends have stopped visiting him in the dorm.* His half of the room is filled with books and papers stacked to the ceiling. He's too "busy" socializing to sort them out. If the campus provided maid service, he would be the first to sign up. Underneath his bed are all of his dirty, smelly clothes from last week. Every Thursday is laundry day for our floor, so at least there is a clear path on the bedroom floor that night. His mother sent him a beautiful bedspread, but it is still in the box because he runs out for class at the last minute every morning and never has time to make the bed.

Brett's slovenliness and laziness tend to irritate me and leave me in a bad mood all day long. Maybe next year I will find a roommate who hates to live in a messy room and who is studying the classics.

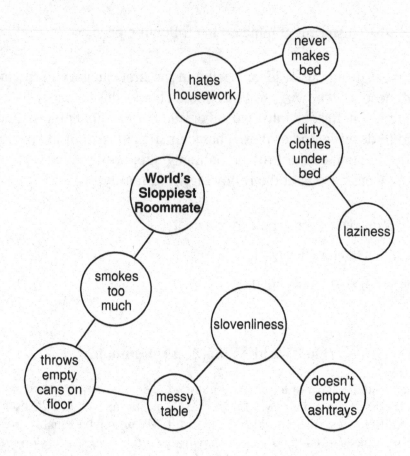

Below is another set of topics. Look at the brainstorming done by one group of students. What additional information can you add to these topics? Try it for the sets of topics that follow, as well.

Television Commercials

cartoon type	too loud
send strong message (drugs, cancer, alcohol)	sensual
picturesque	violent
endorsement by famous people	cute
stupid	disgusting
wild	humorous

_____

_____

A Friend

kind, compassionate

creative

rich

hardworking

gets good grades

giving of himself/herself

intelligent

generous with money

athletic

has own car

humanitarian

dresses well

_____

_____

Music

musicians

radio

solos

playing

types

dances

unusual

concerts

videos

by country

records

instruments

groups

singing

_____

_____

Problems Facing Students

limited funds

tests

assignments

transportation

classes

extracurricular activities

drugs

clothes

career

registration for classes

selection of a school

roommates

peer pressure

alcohol

_____

_____

Brainstorm the following topics, following the examples above:

Extracurricular Activities   Budgeting Time

Part-Time Jobs   Ethnic Foods

Traveling   Buildings on Campus

Cars   Preparing for an Exam

Finding a Job   Importance of Learning English

OUTLINING

An outline is a plan that writers set up to guide them step by step through the writing process. Just as architects draw up blueprints for the construction of buildings, so do writers in preparing for writing compositions. Just as your bones form the skeleton of your body, so does the outline form the skeleton of your writing. Once you have completed the brainstorming process, you will be ready to set up the plan for your essay. As you look at your plan, you can see whether it is logical, chronological, complete, ascending in impact, and detailed. You should consider these points as you are preparing your outline:

- Do all of the main headings pertain to the topic?

- Will the subheadings provide supporting details for the main headings?

- Are there enough supporting details to write an essay with the required number of words? (It is best to determine early in the writing process whether you have the right number of details to fill your paper.)

- Does the outline show how the essay will build from the least to the most important details?

- For a persuasion essay, have you saved your strongest, most convincing details for last?

- Is there a good thesis statement?

- Will the main headings lead to good details?

- Is there a conclusion that lets your readers know that you have said everything and that the essay is complete?

After you have written the outline, you will be able to see at a glance whether your essay will satisfy the requirements of the assignment. It is far better to spend extra time on this phase than to get halfway through the composition only to realize that you have too much or not enough to say about your topic.

Use the following format as a guide.

- The first word of each entry starts with a capital letter.

- Only proper nouns used within the entry require capitals.

- There is no punctuation required unless you choose to use complete sentences.

- There will be, however, a period after each Roman numeral (I. II.), letter (A. B. C. and a. b. c.), or number (1. 2. 3.) in the entry.

- The alignment and indentation of all headings should be consistent.

- Although the thesis statement and the conclusion are not part of the outline, you should include them in the outline so that you can see the total picture at a glance.

Before beginning the exercises in this section on outlining, it would be a good idea to review the concept of *parallel structure*. Outlines, unless very sketchy, need to follow certain patterns, and these rely on the use of parallel structure. As you write a series of elements in any sentence, they must all be in the same format. If you have three or four items and you begin with nouns, you must follow this pattern throughout the outline. Look at the following categories and see how the writer corrected the problems with parallel structure.

Adjectives

INCORRECT: The dress was <u>elegant</u>, <u>flattering</u>, and <u>it fit loosely</u>.

                                     adj.   adj.   S+V+adv.

CORRECT: The dress was <u>elegant</u>, <u>flattering</u>, and <u>loose-fitting</u>.

                                       adj.   adj.   adj.

Adverb

INCORRECT: Gretchen walked <u>gracefully</u> and <u>with care</u> as she crossed the stage.
                              adv.   prep. phrase

CORRECT: Gretchen walked <u>gracefully</u> and <u>carefully</u> as she crossed the stage.
                              adv.   adv.

Gerund

INCORRECT: Misha plans to spend his free time <u>golfing</u>, <u>fishing</u> and
                                                      gerund   gerund

<u>will swim in the pool</u>.
 future prep. phrase

CORRECT: Misha plans to spend his free time <u>golfing</u>, <u>fishing</u>, and <u>swimming</u>.
                                          gerund gerund   gerund

Verb Tense

INCORRECT: We <u>went to the county fair</u>, <u>rode the horses</u>, <u>ate cotton candy</u> and
                      past tense   past tense   past tense

<u>were enjoying the attractions</u>.
 progressive tense

CORRECT: We <u>went to the county fair</u>, <u>rode the horses</u>, <u>ate cotton candy</u>,
                      past tense   past tense   past tense

and <u>enjoyed the attractions</u>.
      past tense.

Mood (all commands)

INCORRECT: <u>Print</u> your address, <u>sign</u> your name, and then <u>you will fold</u>
                  command   command   fut. indic.
            the paper.

CORRECT: <u>Print</u> your address, <u>sign</u> your name, and <u>fold</u> the paper.
              command   command   command

Infinitive

INCORRECT: On their trip to Paris, the Jensens decided <u>to see</u> the sights,
                                                         infinitive

            <u>to attend</u> the opera, <u>and visited</u> the museums.
            infinitive   past tense

CORRECT: On their trip to Paris, the Jensens decided <u>to see</u> the sights,
                                                         infinitive

            <u>to attend</u> the opera, and <u>to visit</u> the museums.
            infinitive   infinitive

Prepositional Phrase

INCORRECT: The kitten chased the ball <u>in the bushes</u>, <u>beside the house</u>,
                                          prep. phrase   prep. phrase

            and <u>it rolled under the car</u>.
                S + V + prep. phrase

CORRECT: The kitten chased the ball <u>in the bushes</u>, <u>beside the house</u>,
                                        prep. phrase   prep. phrase

            and <u>under the car</u>.
                prep. phrase

Many writers prefer informal outlines because they can just set down their ideas without worrying about the format. A few words are sufficient for them to organize their ideas and develop these ideas into a good composition. This type of outline is acceptable in less formal writing, especially when the writers do not need to provide one to their audience. In writing newspaper and magazine articles, short stories, and novels, though these are formal outlets, you do not have to provide an organized plan beforehand. Here is how an informal outline might look.

Your outline could follow any of these patterns, but you must use at least two of each kind of heading (I, II; A, B; 1, 2; a, b).

Thesis Statement	Thesis Statement	Thesis Statement
I.	I.	I.
A.	A.	II.
B.	B.	III.
II.	II.	Conclusion
A.	III.	
1.	A.	
2.	B.	
B.	Conclusion	
III.		
Conclusion		

The following might represent the format for a formal outline.

Thesis Statement:

  I. Main heading 1

    A. Subheading 1

      1. Supporting detail 1

      2. Supporting detail 2

      3. Supporting detail 3

        a. Expanded supporting detail 1

        b. Expanded supporting detail 2

   B. Subheading 2

      1. Supporting detail 1

      2. Supporting detail 2

II. Main heading 2

   A. Subheading 1

   B. Subheading 2

Conclusion:

The essay "Busy Saturdays" has the outline shown below. Although the outline is long, it shows a breakdown of all of the supporting details that the author needed to include in the paragraph. Normally, you would not have to write such a long outline for such a short essay, but even so, it does help in brainstorming and getting the writing to flow. Look at the outline, and then read the paragraph.

Busy Saturdays

Thesis statement: Saturdays are always very busy around our house, and everyone has special chores to do.

  I. Outside Chores

   A. Father's

      1. Cleaning the yard

      2. Repairing broken things

      3. Refinishing furniture

   B. Brother's

      1. Cutting grass

      2. Raking leaves

      3. Trimming hedges

      4. Repairing bicycles

 II. Inside chores

   A. Mother's

      1. Preparing dinner

      2. Working in the kitchen

  B. Mine

     1. Doing the laundry

     2. Ironing

  C. Sister's

     1. Dusting

     2. Vacuuming

     3. Mopping

Conclusion: There is a lot of work for a family of five, and all of us must do our share.

Busy Saturdays

Saturdays are always very busy around our house, and everyone has specific chores to do. My father spends most of his day cleaning up the yard and repairing things that have broken during the week. He also refinishes pieces of furniture that have been scratched. My brother helps him outside. He cuts the grass, rakes the leaves, and trims the hedges. He also repairs our bicycles. My sister and I usually help our mother with the inside work. While our mother prepares the dinner and works in the kitchen, I do all of the laundry and ironing. I hate ironing and sometimes switch jobs with my sister. She takes care of dusting the furniture, vacuuming the carpets, and mopping the floors. There is a lot of work for a family of five, and all of us must do our share.

Look at the content of the following and decide whether the outline would provide the basis for a good essay.

Ways to Save Money

Thesis statement: College students can save money by making a few adjustments in their lifestyles, such as using a different form of transportation, looking for bargains, and altering their attire.

  I. Transportation

  A. Riding a bicycle

  B. Walking

  C. Taking a bus

II. Shopping

    A. Using coupons

    B. Watching for sales

III. Clothing

    A. Sewing at home

    B. Visiting thrift shops

Conclusion: By adjusting their lifestyles and economizing in a variety of ways, college students can save money. Using new means of transportation, having better shopping habits, and altering their clothing tastes will provide them with more money at the end of the month.

One teacher's comment: Nicely organized outline; good thesis statement; three specific ways to save money with supporting details; good rewording of thesis statement.

Preparing for a Career

Thesis statement: Most people hope for successful careers, but they do not realize that it takes a great deal of hard work and education to reach the top.

I. Long-term planning

    A. Goals

    B. Education

    C. Special training

II. Work experience

    A. After-school jobs

    B. Apprenticeships

    C. Long hours

III. Rewards

    A. Job security

    B. Finances

    C. Prestige

Conclusion: People can reap the rewards of success today if they get the proper education and work very hard.

Fast Food Restaurants

Thesis statement: There are three kinds of fast food restaurants: chicken, pizza, and hamburger.

    I. Chicken

        A. Kentucky Fried Chicken

        B. Popeye's

        C. Chicken Delight

    II. Pizza

        A. Pizza Hut

        B. Domino's

        C. Pizza Inn

   III. Hamburger

        A. McDonald's

        B. Wendy's

        C. What-a-Burger

Conclusion: Our town has lots of fast food restaurants. They are all great.

WRITING EXERCISE

Take the following topics and set up a topic outline, following the same format used in the ones above. Include a thesis statement, appropriate subheadings, supporting details, and a conclusion. Brainstorm with other students to come up with as many ideas as possible. Write them out, and then regroup and eliminate the ones you don't need. Once you have finished this process, write a detailed outline as you did for the sample outlines.

Jobs You Have Had	Choosing a Career	Student Expenses
Classmates	Studying for Final Exams	TV Shows
Budgeting Money	A Most Useful Invention	Leisure Activities

Thesis statement:

    I.

      A.

        1.

        2.

      B.

        1.

        2.

    II.

      A.

        1.

        2.

      B.

Conclusion:

WRITING EXERCISE

Using <u>ONE</u> topic from the previous exercise, brainstorm some ideas and write a two-paragraph paper.

PART II
ESL

Advanced Writing

Advanced Writing

ESL

CHAPTER 3
Review of Difficult Grammar Concepts

Chapter 3
Review of difficult grammar concepts

OBJECTIVES FOR DIFFICULT GRAMMAR CONCEPTS

- Learn to combine short, choppy sentences to allow writing to flow smoothly

- Make transitions from one word to a meaningful combination of words

- Recognize run-ons and comma splices and be able to correct them

- Avoid sentence fragments

- Recognize parallel structure in sentences and be able to correct errors

- Avoid grammatical shifts

- Recognize and correct dangling participial modifiers

DANGLING PARTICIPIAL MODIFIERS

Participial phrases are ones that begin with [verb + ing] or [verb + ed] and are not used as subjects. When a participial phrase does not modify the noun or pronoun that usually follows it, it is said to be dangling or just hanging there in the sentence and not modifying the subject of the main clause. The subject of the main clause must be responsible for the two actions, the one in the participle and the one in the main verb.

INCORRECT: *Running down the street*, the taxi passed right by the man.

Running down the street is the participial phrase, but it does not modify the subject, taxi, the word immediately following the phrase. Ask the question: "Was the taxi running down the street?" No, it was the man. Correct the sentence as follows:

CORRECT: Running down the street, the man missed the taxi.

(*He* was running down the street, and he missed the taxi.)

INCORRECT: *Not wanting to disturb anyone*, the shoes were removed before entering the room.

CORRECT: Not wanting to disturb anyone, Tony removed his shoes before entering the room.

or

Because Tony did not want to disturb anyone, he removed his shoes before entering the room.

EXERCISE 23

In the following exercise, select the best sentence in each group to complete the meaning of the sentence and avoid dangling participial modifiers. Write the letter corresponding to the correct choice on the line to the left.

<u>B</u> 1. By using a waterbased paint, ...

A. soap and water will make cleaning up a lot easier.

B. you will find that soap and water make cleaning up a lot easier.

__ 2. When ironing a cotton shirt, ...

A. you will have an easier job if you dampen the material first.

B. the whole operation will be much easier if the shirt has been dampened.

___ 3. Thinking about our place of employment, ...

    A. we must be careful in our selection.

    B. it must be carefully chosen.

___ 4. Having moved to my new neighborhood, ...

    A. I came to enjoy my neighbors' visits.

    B. they made my visit an enjoyable one.

___ 5. When owning a cat or dog, ...

    A. they can be quite expensive.

    B. a person sees the expense involved.

___ 6. Owning either a cat or dog, ...

    A. one has the same expense.

    B. they will both be as expensive.

___ 7. If leaving town for the weekend, ...

    A. pet owners must provide care for their animals.

    B. something has to be done to provide for the animals.

___ 8. After giving the student another chance to prove himself,...

    A. he was dismissed by the principal.

    B. the principal dismissed him.

___ 9. When kissing your date as she gets into the car after smoking, ...

    A. you find that her breath turns you off.

    B. the pleasure of her kiss is affected by the smell of her breath.

___10. With our exercising every day, ...

    A. our circulatory and respiratory systems improve.

    B. we improve our circulatory and respiratory systems.

__11. Growing your own vegetables, ...

    A. they are tastier and more economical.

    B. you enjoy a better flavor and saving money.

__12. By observing any smoker who is out of cigarettes, ...

    A. it is easy to realize how addictive they can be.

    B. one easily realizes how addictive nicotine is.

__13. Feeling sick, ...

    A. the ride down the dusty, bumpy road aggravated my condition.

    B. I became worse while riding down the dusty, bumpy road.

__14. Trying to do her best, ...

    A. Mandy found the job challenging.

    B. the job seemed to be a challenge for Mandy.

__15. Practicing the piano every day, ...

    A. George had decided to follow a musical career.

    B. George's musical career had been chosen.

EXERCISE 24

Decide which of the two sentences is correctly written.

1. A. Selecting the actors very carefully, soap operas count on an excellent crew to make people interested in the show.

  B. Soap opera producers select the actors very carefully to create an interesting show.

2. A. Living alone, it is sad to return to an empty apartment every night.

  B. When one lives alone, it is sad to return to an empty apartment every night.

3. A. Good credit helps people trying to secure a loan.

   B. When trying to finance something, good credit will help the situation.

4. A. A driver cruising at 50 mph will find it difficult to avoid hitting an approaching pedestrian.

   B. If a car is approaching a pedestrian, cruising at 50 mph, it is going to be extremely difficult to avoid hitting him.

5. A. Reading a newspaper will help us learn about international events and their effect on the American economy.

   B. While reading a newspaper, it is easy to learn about international events and their effect on the American economy.

6. A. When driving on the highways, obeying the 65 mph speed limit saves lives.

   B. Drivers should obey the 65 mph speed limit in order to save lives.

7. A. Spectators watched the parachutists perform their stunts while they glided through the sky before gracefully hitting the ground.

   B. Gliding through the sky, the spectators watched the parachutists perform their stunts before gracefully hitting the ground.

8. A. Using an old-fashioned stove, the food won't cook as fast.

   B. Food won't cook as fast on an old-fashioned stove.

9. A. A gardener needs to hoe a great deal in order to grow plants successfully in sandy soil.

   B. Growing plants successfully in sandy soil, the ground has to be hoed a great deal.

10. A. The driver sped down the highway without heeding the speed limit.

    B. Not heeding the speed limit, the car sped down the highway.

11. A. While organizing the new rules for the club, some of the important issues were omitted.

    B. The committee left out some of the important issues while organizing the new rules for the club.

12. A. Torn and faded, Mrs. Sullivan hung the old clothes out to dry.

    B. Mrs. Sullivan hung the old, torn, and faded clothes out to dry.

13. A. Leaning over and dead, the tree surgeon sawed off the decayed branches.

    B. The tree surgeon sawed off the decayed branches of the leaning, dead tree.

14. A. Running down the street, the bus had just pulled away when I arrived.

    B. As I ran down the street, the bus pulled away.

15. A. Hanging crookedly on one hinge, the carpenter replaced the door.

    B. The carpenter replaced the door, which was hanging crookedly on one hinge.

PARALLEL STRUCTURE

It is important that all of the elements of a sentence be parallel. When, for example, you begin to use a series of adjectives in a sentence, make sure that the words you list are all adjectives. Look at these non-parallel sentences and the changes made to correct the errors in them.

> EX: The movie was entertaining, informative, and the scenes were picturesque. (adjective error)
>
> The movie was *entertaining*, *informative*, and *picturesque*.

> EX: The motorist stopped his car, rolled down the window, and asks the policeman what he has done. (verb tense)
>
> The motorist *stopped* his car, *rolled* down the window, and *asked* the policeman what he *had done*.

> EX: Betty loves to read novels, short stories, and books that talk about famous people. (noun error)
>
> Betty loves to read *novels*, *short stories*, and *biographies*.

> EX: During their summer vacation, children love to run, swim, and they have time to relax. (infinitive error)
>
> During their summer vacation, children love to *run*, *swim*, and *relax*.

EX: Buy your pattern and material, lay out the fabric, cut on the lines, and now you are ready to begin sewing the garment. (mood error, imperative to indicative).

Buy your pattern and material, *lay out* the fabric, *cut* on the lines, and *begin* sewing the garment.

EX: Running, jogging, and to swim are good exercises. (gerund error)

Running, *jogging*, and *swimming* are good exercises.

EX: While playing their game, the children hid under the trees, in the bushes, and were behind the buildings. (prepositional phrase error)

While playing their game, the children hid *under the trees*, *in the bushes*, and *behind the building*.

The following coordinating conjunctions require that the constructions that follow them be parallel. Observe the proper placement of the conjunctions.

INCORRECT: Sandy knew not only the president but also visited with his family.

CORRECT: Sandy *not only* knew the president *but also* visited his family. (verb + direct object)

INCORRECT: Irene both speaks Spanish and French.

CORRECT: Irene speaks *both* Spanish *and* French. (noun)

INCORRECT: The Jacksons either plan to live in California or New Mexico.

CORRECT: The Jacksons plan to live *either* in California *or* in New Mexico. (prepositional phrase)

INCORRECT: Joe said that after the war he neither wanted to visit that country nor eat rice.

CORRECT: Joe said that after the war he wanted *neither to visit* that country *nor to eat* rice. (infinitive plus noun)

EXERCISE 25

Look at these sentences and decide whether the elements that are parallel are *nouns, verbs, prepositional phrases, adjectives, gerunds, command forms, or infinitives.*

1. People get emotional, start seeing things, and act crazy on nights when there is a full moon.   **verbs**

2. Television programs regularly entertain, pacify, and frighten children.   **verbs**

3. Before the little boy had crossed the street, he stopped, looked, and listened for cars.

4. The new fast food restaurant serves french fries, shakes, turnovers, and sandwiches.

5. When deciding on a house the buyer must consider three things: size, privacy, and price.

6. Three positive results of good physical fitness are prolonging life, improving appearance, and providing enjoyment.

7. Can you meet the public, be sociable, and stand up for what's right?

8. Since the river was inland, the children had an opportunity to see many different animals, beautiful large trees, and many birds flying in the blue sky dotted with clouds.

9. Take the daily totals, add them together, divide by six, and find your average profits for the week.

10. My favorite pastimes are going to football and basketball games and listening to and playing music.

11. With the cost of living on the rise, and the rapid deflation of the dollar, it is essential for one to work in order to survive.

12. As an athlete, Raúl was powerful, fast, and dynamic.

13. Riding, golfing, and swimming are Dennis' favorite sports.

14. The excited children looked for their Easter eggs under the trees, in the bushes, and on the porch.

15. Monty reads, writes, and speaks English extremely well despite having lived here only a short while.

16. The football players tried to score, tackle, and kick well.

17. Good employees are punctual, dedicated, and hardworking.

18. When taking a test, students must remember to read the questions carefully, to answer correctly, and to check all work before handing it in.

EXERCISE 26

Select the sentence that contains elements of parallel structure. Underline the parallel parts of the sentence.

1. A. The money was found not in the safe, but Jerry finally found it in the drawer.

   B. The money was finally found <u>in the safe</u>, not <u>in the drawer</u>.

2. A. The dog barked, howled, and we saw it run in circles.

   B. The dog <u>barked</u>, <u>howled</u>, and <u>ran</u> in circles.

3. A. When my mother goes on a diet, she always complains about being hungry, tired, or sick to her stomach.

   B. When my mother goes on a diet, she always complains about being hungry, tired, or she has a sick feeling in her stomach.

4. A. I want to work as a banker, property manager, or sell men's wear.

   B. I want to work as a banker, property manager, or salesman.

5. A. Most movie actors are charismatic, handsome, and conceited.

   B. Most movie actors are charismatic, handsome, and a lot seem conceited.

6. A. The cat was always clawing the furniture, teasing the bird, and playing with catnip.

   B. The cat was always clawing the furniture, teased the bird, and played with catnip.

7. A. She ran along the beach, among the sea gulls, and above the pebbles.

   B. She ran along the beach, among the sea gulls, and will clumsily run above the pebbles.

8. A. What do boys know about dresses, dances, and going to the opera?

   B. What do boys know about dresses, dances, and opera?

9. A. The boat was lighter in color, heavier in weight, and the price was very high.

   B. The boat was lighter colored, heavier, and more expensive.

10. A. The woman was attractive, young, and a lot of people knew her.

    B. The woman was attractive, young, and well known.

11. A. She excels in music, in sports, and is pretty smart in math.

    B. She excels in music, sports, and math.

12. A. At the fraternity party, everyone was dancing, drinking, and smoking.

    B. At the fraternity party, everyone was dancing, drinking, and there was a lot of smoke in the air.

13. A. After losing twenty pounds, she looked sick, underweight, and hungry.

    B. After losing twenty pounds, she looked sick, not weighing enough, and hungry.

14. A. While jogging up the hill, she tripped, fell to the ground, and found that she had sprained her ankle.

    B. While jogging up the hill, she tripped, fell, and sprained her ankle.

15. A. If we cut funding for the Thomas Center Gallery, young painters, sculptors, and photographers will lose their exhibition space.

    B. If we cut funding for the Thomas Center Gallery, young painters, those who sculpt, and photographers will lose their only exhibition space.

16. A. Every evening I run, take a swim, or go jogging.

    B. Every evening I run, swim, or jog.

17. A. Misting your ferns makes them full, healthy, and gives them a green color.

    B. Misting your ferns makes them full, healthy, and green.

18. A. The doctor examined the patient, gave a diagnosis, and wrote a bill in fifteen minutes.

    B. The doctor examined the patient, will give a diagnosis, and wrote a bill within a matter of fifteen minutes.

19. A. The small girl could not jump, run, nor will she be able to ski because of her broken foot.

    B. The small girl could not jump, run, nor ski because of her broken foot.

20. A. The millionaire owned many homes, cars, and had a lot of race horses until he went bankrupt.

    B. The millionaire owned many homes, cars, and race horses until he went bankrupt.

SHIFTING

Shifting is the unnecessary changing from one grammatical element to another in a sentence or paragraph. This problem occurs with pronouns, verb tenses, points of view, mood, and active and passive voice. These errors distract readers, and writers must learn to avoid them.

PRONOUN SHIFT involves using a singular pronoun to replace a plural noun or vice-versa.

INCORRECT: <u>Everybody</u> had <u>their</u> hats and coats on and were ready to leave.

CORRECT: <u>Everybody</u> had <u>his/her</u> hat and coat on and was ready to leave.

TENSE SHIFT is the changing from past tense to present or future, from one sentence to another.

INCORRECT: When Mr. Rogers <u>arrived</u> at the airport last night, his family <u>goes</u> to meet him.

CORRECT: When Mr. Rogers <u>arrived</u> at the airport last night, his family <u>went</u> to meet him.

POINT OF VIEW errors occur when there is a shift from indirect speech to direct speech. The same form must be used throughout unless the writer quotes someone's exact words and writes them between quotation marks.

INCORRECT: Philip <u>left</u> to catch his train and then <u>wondered did he pack</u> his wool socks.

CORRECT: Philip <u>left</u> to catch his train and <u>wondered whether he had packed</u> his wool socks.

A common mistake, especially in writing process papers, is to shift from one mood to another (indicative, imperative, or subjunctive). Normally throughout this type of paper, writers use the imperative or command forms because they are trying to get their readers to follow a step-by-step procedure. However, a sudden change to the future tense would create a **MOOD SHIFT.**

INCORRECT: <u>Insert</u> the paper, <u>line up</u> the margins, <u>space down</u> nine times, and <u>you will begin</u> to type.

CORRECT: <u>Insert</u> the paper, <u>line up</u> the margins, <u>space down</u> nine times, and <u>begin</u> to type.

Most writing is in the active voice with the subject performing the action. However, writers can inadvertently shift to the passive voice in the same sentence when someone or something, not the subject, is responsible for the action.

INCORRECT: When I <u>decide</u> to make a dress, I <u>cut out</u> the pattern and then <u>it is sewn</u> together.

CORRECT: When I <u>decide</u> to make a dress, I <u>cut out</u> the pattern and then I <u>sew</u> it together.

EXERCISE 27

Which sentence in each pair below represents a sentence *without* a shift in pronouns?

1. A. Drug abuse can affect a person's mind and body as well as their relationships with their family and friends.

   B. Drug abuse can affect a person's mind and body as well as *his* relationship with *his* family and friends.

2. A. Some medications rob your body of nutrients and then kill your appetite so that you do not want to eat.

   B. Some medications rob your body of nutrients and then kill his appetite so that he does not want to eat.

3. A. Although we drink alcohol to relieve tension, it does numb our minds and make us feel relaxed.

   B. Although we drink alcohol to relieve tension, it does numb a person's mind and make them feel relaxed.

4. A. Violence on children's television programs will confuse their minds and leave them terrified.

   B. Violence on children's television programs will confuse their minds and leave him terrified.

5. A. I came to watch the Super Bowl game, but you could not understand what was going on.

   B. I came to watch the Super Bowl game, but I could not understand what was going on.

6. A. Every person has peers that they admire.

   B. Every person has peers whom he admires.

7. A. A horse can have many shapes and be of a variety of colors, but unlike a cow, they have a mane and a long, flowing tail.

   B. A horse can have many shapes and be of a variety of colors, but unlike a cow, it has a mane and a long, flowing tail.

8. A. Most construction workers work all week long and spend most of their time outdoors.

   B. Most construction workers work all week long, and he spends most of his time outdoors.

9. A. Many people feel that sports are something for enjoyment, while others consider it to be a way of making a living.

   B. Many people feel that sports are for enjoyment, while others consider them to be a way of earning a living.

10. A. Owning a gun, even if guns were outlawed, could be dangerous for many people.

    B. Owning a gun, even if they were outlawed, could be dangerous for many people.

EXERCISE 28

Which sentence in each pair represents a sentence *without* a shift in verb tense?

1. A. The job and the money one earns are the factors that determined which type of neighborhood he chooses.

   B. The job and the money one earns are the factors that determine which neighborhood he chooses.

2. A. When someone thinks about snow skiing, the first thing that came to his mind is the weather.

   B. When someone thinks about snow skiing, the first thing that comes to mind is the weather.

3. A. It was up to the tourist whether he will climb Stone Mountain or not.

   B. It was up to the tourist whether he would climb Stone Mountain or not.

4. A. People who need a diversion from work often spend their evenings getting in shape at a health club.

   B. People who need a diversion from work often spent their evenings getting in shape at a health club.

5. A. In the more than two thousand years since the civilization of man, he has been looking for new and better ways to grow and prepare food.

   B. In the more than two thousand years since the civilization of man, he will be looking for new and better ways to grow and prepare food.

6. A. When a person exercised regularly, he notices his body firming up.

   B. When a person exercises regularly, he notices his body firming up.

7. A. A student can attend classes faithfully and listen carefully, but her attention span had been short.

   B. A student can attend classes faithfully and listen carefully, but her attention span can be short.

8. A. While driving to work last week, Deborah wasn't paying attention and got into an accident.

   B. While driving to work last week, Deborah wasn't paying attention and gets into an accident.

9. A. After he had listened to the music, Gus decides to fix himself a sandwich.

   B. After he had listened to the music, Gus decided to fix himself a sandwich.

10. A. The Little League baseball coach said that his team was ready for the championship game.

    B. The Little League baseball coach said that his team is ready for the championship game.

EXERCISE 29

Which sentence in each pair represents a sentence *without* a shift from active to passive voice?

1. A. Chuck Mangione's music is very soft and mellow and appeals to many appreciative listeners.

   B. Chuck Mangione's music is very soft and mellow and will be heard by many appreciative listeners.

2. A. There are many wealthy cities in America, but even the richest have been affected by inflation.

   B. There are many wealthy cities in America, but inflation has affected even the richest.

3. A. If you watch two musicians for a while, the difference in their styles will be noticed immediately.

   B. If you watch two musicians for a while, you can notice immediately the difference in their styles.

4. A. If you are looking for the best deal on a new car, this can be found at Auto-tron Motors.

   B. If you are looking for the best deal on a new car, shop at Autotron Motors.

5. A. The art world recognizes Salvador Dalí for his wild, surrealist paintings and still exhibits his works.

   B. Salvador Dalí was known for his wild, surrealist paintings and still exhibits his works.

6. A. Football fans can see games on television every Sunday from September to January and can watch baseball from April to October.

   B. Football games are seen on television every Sunday from September to January, while we can watch baseball from April to October.

7. A. The wind was blowing fiercely and the leaves were swept away.

   B. The wind was howling and the leaves were blowing away.

8. A. Someone tried to force his way into the Roths' house, but he was shot by the owner.

   B. Someone tried to force his way into the Roths' house, but the owner shot him.

9. A. While you are in the pharmacy, medicine could be bought for my cold.

   B. While you are in the pharmacy, you could buy medicine for my cold.

10. A. If you follow the easy instructions, you will finish the table in no time.

    B. If you follow the easy instructions, the table will be finished in no time.

EXERCISE 30

Which sentence in each pair represents a sentence *without* a shift in point of view?

1. A. Even though Jacques was nominated for the award, he wondered how long it would take to receive it.

   B. Even though Jacques was nominated for the award, he wondered will he be receiving it soon.

2. A. As Rick pulled off the road to fix his flat tire, he wondered is the spare in good condition.

   B. As Rick pulled off the road to fix his flat tire, he wondered if the spare was in good condition.

3. A. Almost anyone can take pictures, but he wonders if they will turn out well.

   B. Almost anyone can take pictures, but he wonders will they turn out well.

4. A. Sonia wants another piece of cake, but she thinks she will get fat by eating it.

   B. Sonia wants another piece of cake, but she thinks will I get fat by eating it.

5. A. One must ski for the pleasure it affords without thinking will I get hurt on the slopes.

   B. One must ski for the pleasure it affords without thinking whether he will get hurt on the slopes.

6. A. Everyone should bolt his door at night and not have to worry will someone try to break in.

   B. Everyone should bolt his door at night and not have to worry whether someone will try to break in.

7. A. In questioning the witnesses, the prosecutor asked were you at the dance on the night of the murder.

   B. In questioning the witnesses, the prosecutor asked if they had been at the dance on the night of the murder.

8. A. The food in the cafeteria leaves a lot to be desired and everyone wonders why don't they provide something better.

   B. The food in the cafeteria leaves a lot to be desired and everyone wonders why the cafeteria doesn't provide something better.

9. A. We have called Kyle twice today without being able to speak to him and wonder can he be sick.

   B. We have called Kyle twice today without being able to speak to him and wonder if he is sick.

10. A. I used a new wax on my floor and wondered if it would be better than the other one.

    B. I used a new wax on my floor and wonder will it be better than the other one.

EXERCISE 31

Which sentence in each pair represents a sentence *without* a mood shift?

1. A. Dig the hole, plant the seed, and then you will have to water it daily.

   B. Dig the hole, plant the seed, and water it daily.

2. A. Guido wrote the words and the music to his own song, but don't sing it.

   B. Guido, write the words and the music to your own song, but don't sing it.

3. A. The coach said, "Run around the track, do push-ups, and we will meet here at 4:30."

   B. The coach said, "Run around the track, do push-ups, and meet here at 4:30."

4. A. The physician insisted that his patient quit smoking, eat less, and he should get more exercise.

   B. The physician insisted that his patient quit smoking, eat less, and get more exercise.

5. A. Place the nail over the area you wish to join, hit it hard with the hammer a number of times, and after that you need to cover the hole with putty, and paint it.

   B. Place the nail over the area you wish to join, hit it hard with the hammer a number of times, cover the hole with putty, and paint it.

6. A. After you have lined up all the ingredients, mix the batter, place it in a pan, and now you are ready to set it in the oven to bake.

   B. After you have lined up all the ingredients, mix the batter, place it in a pan, and set it in the oven to bake.

7. A. Probing deeper into the water, the pearl diver finds a large oyster, pries it open, and gives it to a waiting customer.

   B. Probing deeper into the water, the pearl diver finds a large oyster, pries it open, and might give it to a waiting customer.

8. A. Drag out the lawn mower, fill it with gas, pull the cord, and cut the grass.

   B. Drag out the lawn mower, fill it with gas, pull the cord; now you are ready to cut the grass.

9. A. After covering all the furniture with drop cloths, the painter taped up the window frames and took down the curtains; now paint the room with the roller.

   B. After covering all the furniture with drop cloths, the painter taped up the window frames took down the curtains, and painted the room with the roller.

10. A. The lawyer insisted that his client write down all the information; provide names, places, and dates; and he has to tell the truth.

    B. The lawyer insisted that his client write down all the information; provide names, places, and dates; and tell the truth.

EXERCISE 32

Circle the correctly written sentence in each group.

1. A. Whenever one is driving on the highway, you should be careful.

   B. Whenever you are driving on the highway, you should be careful.

   C. Whenever one is driving on the highway, they should be careful.

2. A. Bait the hook, cast the line, now you are ready for the fish to bite.

   B. Bait the hook, cast the line, and wait for the fish to bite.

   C. You can bait the hook, cast the line, and you will wait for the fish to bite.

3. A. Having a pet, a dog or cat can provide a lasting friendship.

   B. Deciding to own a pet, we can enjoy a lasting friendship.

   C. Deciding to own a pet, a lasting friendship can be enjoyed.

4. A. I want a thick, rich, and creamy milk shake.

   B. I want a thick, rich milk shake that is creamy.

   C. I want a thick, creamy milk shake with lots of flavor.

5. A. If everyone takes their time and shops around, they will find many bargains.

   B. If everyone takes one's time and shops around, one will find many bargains.

   C. If everyone takes his time and shops around, he will find many bargains.

6. A. The young boy never told anyone why he is saving his money.

   B. The young boy never told anyone why he was saving his money.

   C. The young boy never told anyone why he will be saving his money.

7. A. The hotel where we stayed was clean, affordable, and had a central location.

   B. The hotel where we stayed was clean, affordable, and it was close to everything.

   C. The hotel where we stayed was clean, had a good price, and was easy to get to.

8. A. I got lost in the bus station because it is so big, there were lots of people, and it was unfamiliar.

   B. I got lost in the bus station because it was very large, many people were there, and because it was unfamiliar.

   C. I got lost in the bus station because it was so big, crowded, and unfamiliar.

9. A. The guinea pig scampered in the leaves, under the sofa, and over the desk.

   B. The guinea pig scampered among the leaves, went over the chair, and he hid under the bookcase.

   C. The guinea pig hid under the sofa; he went in the closet; and finally behind the boxes.

10. A. Sorting out the nails, the hammer was used to pound them.

    B. Sorting out the nails, the carpenter found the ones he needed.

    C. Sorting out the nails, the board was nailed in place.

11. A. Typing as fast as she could, the secretary finished the letters just at quitting time.

    B. Typing as fast as she could, the boss complimented the secretary for a job well done.

    C. Typing as fast as she could, the letters went out in the evening mail.

12. A. Go straight ahead two blocks, turn left, and then you will see the museum.

    B. Go straight ahead two blocks, turn left, and look for museum on your right.

    C. Go straight ahead two blocks, turn left, and the museum will be on your right.

13. A. All the students turned in their essays after writing it.

    B. All the students turned in their essays after they had written them.

    C. All the students turned in their essays after they wrote them.

14. A. The president cut spending, raised taxes, and will try to balance the budget.

    B. The president cut spending, raised taxes, and balanced the budget.

    C. The president cut spending, has raised taxes, and will balance the budget.

15. A. Many times during your life, we can have unforeseen expenses.

    B. Many times during your life, you can have unforeseen expenses.

    C. Many times during one's life, they can have unforeseen expenses.

16. A. How often you study, not how long, determines how well you will do in this class.

    B. How often you study, not the time that you spend, determines how well you did in this class.

    C. If you study a lot, not how many hours, determines how well you will do in this class.

17. A. Always carry a spare tire, a jack for emergency use, and something to gauge air pressure.

    B. Always carry a spare tire, a jack, and gauge the tire pressure.

    C. Always carry a spare tire, a jack, and a pressure gauge.

18. A. Writing so many essays, my pen ran out of ink.

    B. Having written so many essays, my pen ran out of ink.

    C. After I had written so many essays, my pen ran out of ink.

19. A. While waiting for the train, I met an interesting man.

    B. While waiting for the train, an interesting man jumped off and started to talk to me.

    C. While waiting for the train, my luggage got lost.

20. A. Lou completed his chores, prepared lunch, and then he was relaxing.

    B. Lou completed his chores, was preparing lunch, and then he was relaxing.

    C. Lou completed his chores, prepared lunch, and then relaxed.

RUN-ONS AND COMMA SPLICES

Two common punctuation errors are run-ons and comma splices. **Run-ons** are two complete sentences joined without the use of commas, semicolons, or conjunctions. **Comma splices** are two complete sentences joined by a comma just like joining (splicing) two pieces of film or tape that have become torn. Both errors can be corrected by using a subordinate clause (review chapter in this unit), or a comma followed by a conjunction. You can also eliminate the subject of the second sentence and join the two clauses with a conjunction. If both sentences are long, then a semicolon can be used and no conjunction is required to connect them. A period can be used to form two sentences.

RUN-ON: Marcia went to the store she bought all the food she needed for the party.

CORRECT: *When Marcia went to the store, she bought all the food she needed for the party.* (subordinate clause)

Marcia went to the store and bought all the food she needed for the party. (eliminate subject and use conjunction)

Marcia went to the store, and she bought all the food she needed for the party. (use comma and conjunction)

LONG RUN-ON: Last summer while we were on vacation, we saw many indigenous people living on the mountain slopes of the Andes they were wearing very brightly colored multilayered clothing.

CORRECT: *While on vacation last summer, we saw many indigenous people living on the mountain slopes of the Andes. They were wearing very brightly colored multilayered clothing*

COMMA SPLICE: The boys went to the beach, they swam for hours.

CORRECTED: *The boys went to the beach and swam for hours.* (eliminate subject and use conjunction)

The boys went to the beach, and they swam for hours. (use comma and conjunction)

While the boys were at the beach, they swam for hours. (subordinate clause)

LONG COMMA SPLICE: The entomologist conducted investigations in Latin America, his research led to many cures for diseases.

CORRECT: *The entomologist conducted investigations in Latin America; his research led to many cures for diseases.*

COMMA SPLICE: Ted earned good grades in high school, he won a college scholarship.

CORRECT: *Ted earned good grades in high school; he won a college scholarship.*

After earning good grades in high school, Ted won a college scholarship.

COMMA SPLICE: It was raining there was a traffic jam we arrived late.

CORRECT: We arrived late because of the rain and a traffic jam.

We arrived late because of a traffic jam caused by the rain.

COMMA SPLICE: I read a magazine article about cholesterol then I changed my eating habits.

CORRECT: *I changed my eating habits after reading an article about cholesterol.*

EXERCISE 33

Decide whether the following are run-ons (R) or comma splices (CS). Underline the part of the sentence where the error occurs.

1. Growing your own vegetables not only gives you personal satisfaction it also saves a lot of money. *R* when growing your own ... , it also

2. At the beginning of the firearms era, guns were used for hunting and for sport, now they are used mainly to kill people. *R*

3. You will need a lot of light to take outdoor pictures, a good sunny day will do.

4. When jogging, pay attention to your body, it will let you know when you have found a distance that will be comfortable.

5. Don't worry changing your own tire it can be done easily.

6. Just about every child has a favorite book, he likes having someone read it to him.

7. Don't just think about these things do them.

8. Customers can examine the products of glass containers however they can only hope for quality in the contents of metal cans.

9. Depression actually occurs, it is caused by severe problems and must be faced honestly.

10. This new diet has one of the easiest and simplest plans for an individual to follow, for example, there are no pills, drugs, or calories to count.

11. Slalom skiing is like riding a bike once a person knows how, he will never forget it.

12. The horse's face is beautiful and very sweet it is long and narrow with a square jaw.

13. Becoming healthy is not a difficult task it just takes time.

14. Melanie probably does not stay at home, in fact, she might do a lot of traveling for her company.

15. Being lonely is no fun at all, people should enjoy loving companionship throughout their lives.

16. No longer was America worried about Asia, it had a war of unbelievable proportions right here on its doorstep.

17. Credit cards are small and compact, they are trim and easy to hold.

18. Police cruise neighborhoods looking for speeders it is their job to ticket the violators.

19. Water is a very versatile thing, it revives, refreshes, and nourishes every living thing.

20. Government reports show that population growth has to be controlled, if not, it will harm the family, the government, and society.

EXERCISE 34

Decide whether the following are comma splices (CS) or run-ons (R). Underline the part of the sentence where the error occurs.

1. A football is <u>oval, most</u> often it is made of pigskin.   *CS*

2. Many students attend classes to learn a trade or become <u>professionals others</u> go to have fun.   *R*

3. One kind of football fan never sits during a game, he just walks around the stadium.

4. German shepherds don't even fuss when a person corrects them they seem to understand.

5. The Landmark Apartments not only have no attached patios they don't even provide a place to enjoy the outdoors.

6. After sitting for six hours in the direct sunlight, a lifeguard is far from tanned, he is burned.

7. There are also skin- and scuba-diving trips organized for tourists, they can see the most beautiful coral reefs.

8. It never fails, she smokes a cigarette when I am around.

9. On the lens of a camera there is a diaphragm it operates like the human eye.

10. If you have not run in a long time, start out slowly and go only short distances, this will build up your endurance.

11. Learning to play chess is not very difficult like anything else, it just takes lots of practice.

12. The hostess prepared a gourmet meal her guests enjoyed the Asian dishes.

13. Classical music provides the listener with relaxing melodies it soothes inner tension.

14. Shopping at the new mall is a pleasure there are many different stores under the same roof.

15. No one saw the train leave the tracks it was all so sudden.

16. My friend won a Caribbean cruise she is leaving next month.

17. The committee informed Michael of his scholarship, he would begin classes immediately.

18. Near the coast sailing boats are cruising, the boaters can see the sea floor without diving into the water.

19. The flower exhibition was magnificent there were many colorful and exotic arrangements.

20. Hang gliding is a difficult sport it requires hand and eye coordination as well as skill.

EXERCISE 35

Correct the following run-on sentences.

1. My sister is studying chemistry, **_and_** she hopes to become a famous scientist.

2. The windows of the cottage were dark. **_W_** ~~w~~here was the rest of the family?

3. We rode until nearly dark then we raced home to supper.

4. He is an excellent dentist he has a large office downtown.

5. Much depends upon your help you won't fail us, will you?

6. We planned the design and carried it out on the leather this took real skill.

7. Our parents went to New York they went to visit relatives.

8. All materials are similar in certain ways they may not look or feel alike.

9. Electric current is not a material it does not take up space.

10. There are three states of matter material is another name for matter.

11. He rested for two hours he then felt better.

12. The children ran into the street heedlessly they never stopped to look either way.

13. The committee decided to hold a dance there would be an admission charge of one dollar.

14. The canoe plunged through the dangerous rapids water splashed the occupants.

15. On my new skis I have fallen many times I keep trying.

16. Let's have lamb chops I'm tired of roast beef.

17. He attended high school in Denver then his family moved to Seattle.

18. Do you think it will rain that will spoil our fun.

19. Please go to bed it is getting late.

20. The trees were bare of leaves how could it be summer?

SENTENCE COMBINING

Reading anything with many short, choppy sentences one right after the other is boring and causes readers to lose interest. Writers should vary the length of their sentences, making some long and others short. You can combine many shorter sentences by using the subordinate conjunctions indicated in this section or by adding the following conjunctions: *and, by, for, nor, or, so,* or *yet. Do not be afraid to eliminate excess words.* Rearrange the order, or change the words, but do not lose sight of the original meaning. Look at the following examples to see how writers eliminated excess words.

I know a good restaurant. It serves only pizza. The prices are low.

I know a good, inexpensive pizza restaurant.

All months have at least 28 days. February has only 28 days. It is the shortest.

February is the shortest month, with only 28 days.

We drove out West last summer. We saw many mountains. They were very picturesque.

Last summer we drove out West and saw many picturesque mountains.

Most native speakers of English prefer shorter, simpler language in writing. By doing so, they reduce and/or eliminate excessive wordiness. Even so, short sentences are combined whenever possible to improve the flow of ideas in the essay.

EXERCISE 36

In the following, decide whether sentence A or sentence B is the better combination of the original short, choppy sentences. Avoid verbosity.

1. The child is playing with a toy. The toy is a red ball. The ball is big.

   A. The child is playing with a red ball that is big.

   B. The child is playing with a big red ball.

2. Lonnie likes to fish. He catches many bass. He goes to Lake Santa Fe.

   A. Lonnie likes to fish because he catches many bass when he goes to Lake Santa Fe.

   B. Lonnie catches a lot of bass in Lake Santa Fe.

3. There are flowers in the vase. They are roses and carnations. The vase is on the table.

   A. There are flowers in the vase that are roses and carnations on the table.

   B. There are roses and carnations in the vase on the table.

4. The television does not work well. There is a short circuit. I can't watch my favorite program.

   A. Because there is a short circuit and the television does not work well, I can't watch my favorite program.

   B. I can't watch my favorite program because there is a short circuit in the television.

5. Buddy hit a home run. It was his twentieth of the season. He was very proud.

   A. Buddy was so proud because he hit a home run, and it was his twentieth of the season.

   B. Buddy was so proud when he hit his twentieth home run of the season.

6. The patio is nice. It overlooks a lovely garden. The garden is colorful.

   A. The nice patio overlooks a lovely garden that is colorful.

   B. The nice patio overlooks a lovely colorful garden.

7. Doris's dog has fleas. He wears a collar. It protects him against them.

   A. Doris's dog wears a flea collar to protect him.

   B. Even though Doris's dog wears a flea color, it protects him.

8. We are planning to fly to Wyoming tomorrow. You must not get up late. You have to finish packing your bags. We'll be upset if you're late.

   A. We'll be upset if you don't finish packing your bags and get up early enough to catch the flight to Wyoming tomorrow.

   B. You must not get up late tomorrow because we are flying to Wyoming and you have to finish packing your bags or else we'll be upset if you are late.

9. Jonathan can't buy the car. He looked at it last week. It's a new red sports model. It's because he doesn't have the money.

   A. Jonathan can't buy the car that he looked at last week because it is a new red sports model and he does not have the money.

   B. Because he doesn't have the money, Jonathan can't buy the new red sports car that he looked at last week.

10. The tourists went to Niagara Falls. They saw many beautiful colors. They were reflected on the water at night. It was like a rainbow.

   A. The tourists who went to Niagara Falls saw a rainbow of colors reflected on the water at night.

   B. The tourists went to Niagara Falls because they wanted to see many beautiful rainbow colors reflected in the night waters.

EXERCISE 37

Which of these pairs of sentences is written correctly? Avoid verbosity.

1. Baked potatoes are good for you. They are high in fiber. They have few calories.

   A. Baked potatoes are good for you because they are high in fiber and low in calories.

   B. Since baked potatoes are good for you, they are high in fiber and low in calories.

2. Harry likes to play tennis. It helps him relieve tension.

   A. Because Harry wants to relieve tension, he likes to play tennis to do it.

   B. Harry likes to play tennis because it helps him relieve tension.

3. Sam wanted to make a jewelry box. He bought the wood. Then he purchased the tools.

   A. Sam wanted to make a jewelry box, so he bought some wood and tools.

   B. Sam bought some wood and tools to make a jewelry box.

4. There was a terrible drought during the summer. The crops died. Farmers lost a lot of money.

   A. Last year's terrible summer drought killed the crops and cost farmers a lot of money.

   B. There was a terrible drought last summer that killed the crops and cost farmers a lot of money.

5. Many students do not like poetry. It is difficult to read. It is also difficult to understand.

   A. Many students do not like poetry because it is difficult to read and understand.

   B. Poetry is so difficult to read and understand, and that is why many students do not like it.

6. Photography is a wonderful art. It is an expression of the photographer. Each photographer is unique.

   A. Photography is a wonderful art that is an expression of the photographer who is unique.

   B. Photography is a wonderful art that is a unique expression of the photographer.

7. St. Augustine is in Florida. It was the first permanent colony in the United States. The Spanish colonized it. It was also under French and British rule.

   A. St. Augustine, Florida, the first permanent Spanish colony in the United States, was also ruled by the French and British.

   B. St. Augustine is Florida's first permanent colony in the United States, colonized by the Spanish and ruled by the English and French.

8. Nevada is a state in the western part of our country. Las Vegas is famous for its casinos. Many tourists go there hoping to win a lot of money.

   A. Many tourists go to Las Vegas, hoping to win a lot of money in the casinos in Nevada which are located in the western part of the country.

   B. Many tourists go to Las Vegas, Nevada, in the western part of the country, hoping to win a lot of money in the casinos.

9. Squirrels are small animals with long, bushy tails. They are members of the rodent family. They live in trees. Nuts and fruits are foods that they eat.

   A. Squirrels, members of the rodent family, have long, bushy tails, live in trees, and eat nuts and fruits.

   B. Squirrels that live in trees, are members of the rodent family, eat nuts and fruits, and have long, bushy tails.

10. Lightning kills many people every year. They stand under trees when it is raining. Trees get struck by lightning and fall on people.

    A. Every year lightning kills many people who stand under trees when it is raining.

    B. When it is raining, many people stand under trees, and then they get killed when lightning strikes the trees.

11. Sylvia has a garden. It is lovely. It is very fragrant. There are many flowers in it. There are many different colors, too.

   A. Sylvia has a lovely and fragrant garden filled with many colored flowers.

   B. Sylvia has a garden that is filled with many different flowers that are lovely and smell nice.

12. Big cars are not practical. They waste a lot of gasoline. They are expensive.

   A. Big cars are expensive and waste gasoline, and that makes them not practical.

   B. Big cars are not practical because they are expensive and waste gasoline.

13. Washington, D.C., is the capital of the United States. It became the capital in 1800. It was once burned by the British.

   A. After Washington, D.C., became the capital of the United States in 1800 and was burned by the British.

   B. The British burned Washington, D.C., after it became the capital in 1800.

14. Aaron Burr was an American politician. He shot Alexander Hamilton in a duel. He died.

   A. Aaron Burr, an American politician, shot and killed Alexander Hamilton in a duel.

   B. Aaron Burr was an American politician who shot Alexander Hamilton in a duel and that killed him.

15. Many people like to ski. It is fun. They like the feeling of moving quickly down the slopes.

   A. Many people like to ski because it is fun, and they like the feeling of moving quickly down the slopes.

   B. Skiing is fun and gives a feeling of moving quickly down the slopes and that's what makes people like it so much.

CHAPTER REVIEW EXERCISE

Read the following passage and answer the questions that follow. Select the best answer for each statement. Some sentences may be correct.

(1) Archery is a wonderful sport that the whole family from 8 to 80 years can enjoy. (2) Every year there is numerous competitions throughout the United States. (3) In some 35 states, people hunt and fish with bow and arrow. (4) The sport has acquired such high status that in 1972 some people even won gold medals in the Olympics. (5) There are not a lot of equipment necessary for this sport, but the bows and arrows can be expensive. (6) A much more expensive and very powerful bow is the crossbow, some with 150-pound draw weight. (7) There are also compound hunting bows with adjustable draw weights from 45 to 70 pounds, which are made of aluminum or laminated wood.

(8) They either have aluminum or wood shafts with plastic fletchings and specially made tips for either target shooting or hunting.

(9) Participants can avoid accidents by taking the following precautions shoot only at the target; never draw or shoot when someone is between you and your target; always be sure that no one is behind your target. (10) Never shoot up in the air or aim in any direction where you might destroy a living thing; never shoot your bow without an arrow in it; if an arrow has even a small crack, throw it away immediately. (11) An archery set is not a toy, so treat it with respect and have a safe and enjoyable family outing.

1. **Sentence 1: Archery is a wonderful sport that the whole family from 8 to 80 years can enjoy.**

   What correction should be made to this sentence?

   A. insert <u>of age</u> after <u>years</u>

   B. omit <u>that</u>

   C. change <u>from</u> to <u>ranging from</u>

2. **Sentence 2: Every year there is numerous competitions throughout the United States.**

   What correction should be made to this sentence?

   A. change <u>is</u> to <u>are</u>

   B. insert a comma after <u>competition</u>

   C. omit <u>the</u>

3. **Sentence 3: In some 35 states, people hunt and fish with bow and arrow.**

   What correction should be made to this sentence?

   A. change <u>people</u> to <u>People</u>

   B. insert a comma after <u>fish</u>

   C. insert <u>a</u> before <u>bow</u>

4. **Sentences 2 and 3: Every year there is numerous competitions throughout the United States. In some 35 states, people hunt and fish with bow and arrow.**

   The most effective combination would be

   A. States, when

   B. Sates, in which some

   C. States, and in some

5. **Sentence 5: There are not a lot of equipment necessary for this sport, but the bows and arrows can be expensive.**

   What corrections should be made to this sentence?

   A. change <u>are</u> to <u>is</u>

   B. omit the comma before <u>but</u>

   C. change <u>can be</u> to <u>are</u>

6. **Sentence 6: A much more expensive and very powerful bow is the <u>cross-bow, some with</u> 150-pound draw weight.**

   Which of the following is the best way to write the underlined portion of the sentence? If you think the original is the best way, choose option (A).

   A. crossbow, some with

   B. crossbow. Some with

   C. crossbow; some have a

7. **Sentence 7: There are also compound hunting bows with adjustable draw weights from 45 to 70 pounds, which are made of aluminum or laminated wood.**

   What correction should be made to this sentence?

   A. change <u>are</u> to <u>is</u>

   B. insert a comma after <u>bows</u>

   C. insert a comma after <u>aluminum</u>

8. **Sentence 8: They either have aluminum or wood shafts with plastic fletch-ings and specially made tips for either target shooting or hunting.**

   What correction should be made to this sentence?

   A. change <u>either have</u> to <u>have either</u>

   B. change <u>and</u> to <u>or</u>

   C. change <u>specially</u> to <u>especially</u>

9. **Sentence 9: Participants can avoid accidents by taking the following <u>precautions shoot</u> only at the target; never draw or shoot when someone is between you and your target; always be sure that no one is behind your target.**

   Which of the following is the best way to write the underlined portion of the sentence? If you think the original is the best way, choose option (A).

   A. precautions shoot

   B. precautions, shoot

   C. precautions: shoot

10. **Sentence 10: Never shoot up in the air or aim in any direction where you might destroy a living thing; never shoot your bow without an arrow in it; if an arrow has even a small crack, throw it away immediately.**

   What correction should be made to this sentence?

   A. change <u>it</u> to <u>them</u>

   B. omit comma after <u>crack</u>

   C. change <u>it; if</u> to <u>it. If</u>

   Read the following passage and answer the questions that follow. Select the best answer for each statement. Some sentences may be correct.

   (1) Young people today can save money by making a few adjustments in their lifestyles. (2) Using different forms of transportation, looking for bargains, and altering their attire are three ways to begin. (3) Riding a bicycle and walking are two economical and very healthy ways to change their lifestyles. (4) This method saves on gas, auto repairs, and insurance premiums. (5) Taking a bus also allows them to read, write, or study while someone else watch the road. (6) Using coupons to offset purchases can save an average of $10 or more per week.

(7) Watching for sales on higher-priced merchandise can greatly lower expenditures. (8) Young people can also have fun while bargain hunting at neighborhood garage and church rummage sails. (9) Visiting local thrift shops will help them find special bargains even on brand-new clothes or articles for the house. (10) Making some of these changes can provide many benefits. (11) New means of transportation, better shopping habits, and altering their clothing purchases will provide them with more money at the end of the month and make them more healthier.

11. **Sentence 2: Using different forms of transportation, looking for bargains, and altering their attire are three ways to begin.**

    What correction should be made to this sentence?

    A. change <u>are</u> to <u>is</u>

    B. change <u>to begin</u> to for <u>beginning</u>

    C. no correction is necessary

12. **Sentence 3: Riding a bicycle and walking are two economical and very healthy ways to change their lifestyles.**

    What correction should be made to this sentence?

    A. change <u>is</u> to <u>are</u>

    B. change <u>healthy</u> to <u>healthier</u>

    C. no correction is necessary

13. **Sentence 5: Taking a bus also allows them to read, write, or study while someone else watch the road.**

    What correction should be made to this sentence?

    A. insert a comma after <u>bus</u>

    B. change <u>watch</u> to <u>watches</u>

    C. change <u>taking</u> to <u>to take</u>

14. Sentence 8: Young people can also have fun while bargain hunting at neighborhood garage and church rummage sails.

What correction should be made to this sentence?

A. change <u>sails</u> to <u>sales</u>

B. change <u>while</u> to <u>when they</u>

C. change <u>young people</u> to <u>they</u>

15. Sentence 9: Visiting local thrift shops will help them find special bargains even on brand-new clothes or articles for the house.

What correction should be made to this sentence?

A. insert a comma after <u>shops</u>

B. insert a comma before <u>even</u>

C. change <u>for</u> to <u>of</u>

16. Sentence 11: New means of transportation, better shopping habits, and altering their clothing purchases will provide them with more money at the end of the month and make them more healthier.

What correction should be made to this sentence?

A. change <u>provide them</u> to <u>provide young people</u>

B. change <u>make them more healthier</u> to <u>enable them to become healthier</u>

C. no correction is necessary

Advanced Writing

ESL

CHAPTER 4

Making the Transition from Paragraphs to Essays

Chapter 4

Making the transition from paragraphs to essays

It is time to make the transition from writing paragraphs to writing essays. The process is not difficult, but it requires more concentration, brainstorming, and revising. As it took time to make all sentences relate to the topic and to the topic sentence, it now takes time to relate the information in the paragraphs to the topic expressed in the thesis statement. This process involves exhausting *all* possibilities in your brainstorming. It also forces you to focus on one aspect of the topic and not allow yourself to write on just anything that comes into your mind.

Now you need to select a broader topic than before. Make sure that it is not too broad, however, or you will have to include more information than you can cover in an essay. In eliminating some information in the brainstorming process, regroup all of the ideas into two or three categories. These will provide you with the information for developing the three paragraphs of the body of the essay. As you look at the regrouped ideas, you will be able to decide whether you have enough material for an essay. If you do not, either try to brainstorm to get more ideas or select another topic. If you try to write immediately, you may not have enough time to think about another topic. Look for a main idea for each paragraph, but be sure that it relates to the thesis statement. Then write the topic sentence to which all of the sentences in the paragraph will relate.

WHAT DOES AN ESSAY LOOK LIKE?

In an essay, the paragraphs are longer and there are more of them. Now you need at least five paragraphs instead of one, a thesis statement, three topic sentences, and more supporting details. As you write all paragraphs except the first and last, you must begin with a topic sentence and make sure that all of the other sentences in that paragraph relate to it. Look at everything and be sure that it relates to the thesis statement from the beginning paragraph. The thesis statement itself and the conclusion are not necessarily longer than in a paragraph essay, but the paragraphs containing them will be.

Everyone's Advice

Thesis Statement: Before I leave for my "big adventure," parents, friends, and relatives all offer advice on what to do and how to act, what to wear, and how to succeed.

I. What Not to Do and How to Act

Not to A. Drink too much

Not to B. Be too friendly with strangers

C. Become a failure   *If she did not study hard*

D. Lose face   →

E. Be a disappointment   *the teacher would be disappointed*

II. What to Wear

A. To class   *Not to use blue jeans and sweatshirts*

B. To parties   *Not ruffled party dresses (more serious)*

III. How to Succeed

A. Compromise on clothes   *She didn't want to be different from everyone else*

B. Learn to budget time

Conclusion: Despite my initial frustrations, I found that I could listen to everyone's advice, use my own good judgment, and still be a success.

Notice how the writer of the essay divided the thesis statement into three components: what to do and how to act, what to wear, and how to succeed. From each of these ideas a topic sentence and a paragraph with details that support it will be created. All of the ideas in the supporting paragraphs, in turn, reinforce the thesis statement. By expanding on the thesis statement, writers inform their readers of the ideas that will appear in the essay. The thesis statement, in this way, sets up a plan for you to follow when you are developing the essay.

Many introductory paragraphs, such as the one in the essay on the next page, provide some background information on the topic before presenting the thesis statement. The introductory paragraph uses key words and phrases that indicate the method that the writer will use to develop the essay. These methods including narrative, descriptive, process, comparison/contrast, and persuasion, and they will all be discussed at length in the following sections.

As you begin a writing assignment, reserve enough time for brainstorming. Coming up with the information for all of the details you want to include in your essay will require much thought. You will then have to re-group your ideas and possibly eliminate some, being careful to include only those that develop the main idea of each paragraph.

Keep These Points in Mind As You Prepare to Write

- Don't worry about correcting grammar until you have finished writing.

- Get your ideas down on paper first.

- Organize your ideas.

- Make sure that each sentence contains a complete idea.

- Don't begin every sentence with the same words.

- Indent all new paragraphs.

- Always double-space between lines so that your instructor can insert comments.

- Skip one line between each line that you write longhand.

- Write from five- to seven-sentence paragraphs, depending on the length of the sentences and how much information required to completely develop the topic.

- Avoid writing fragments.

- Use transition words effectively so that you guide your reader smoothly from one idea to the next.

- Concentrate on varying the length of the sentences.

- Edit your paper for mistakes in vocabulary, grammar, and form.

    Look at the student essay that follows. Notice the format, thesis statement, topic sentences, details, transition words, and conclusion.

Everyone's Advice

    People in today's world are more mobile than they used to be. Students have greater opportunities to travel and to study abroad than ever before. *Before they leave for their "big adventure," parents, friends, and relatives all offer advice on what to do and how to act, what to wear, and how to succeed.* } background } thesis statement

    Before I left my country, my family told me more of what not to do than what I should do. My mother told me not to drink too much because I would betray my heritage. Then my father told me not to be too friendly with strangers. He also warned me that if I did not study hard, I would be a failure and lose face among family and friends. Furthermore, my teachers would be disappointed in me. My friends warned me about driving in heavy traffic. I began to wonder whether studying abroad would be a good idea. However, several of my friends who had visited the country before began to tell me about all the exciting places to visit and how warm and wonderful the people were. Finally, I began to feel more comfortable about my big adventure. } topic statement } transition words support

    Besides that advice, everyone had a different idea of what I should wear for every occasion. As I packed my bags, I became frustrated because my parents felt that blue jeans and sweatshirts were not appropriate clothes to wear to class. A short time later when I selected a ruffled party dress, my mother cried for days. Not wanting to cause problems, I exchanged these clothes for something more serious. Was I surprised my first day of classes when many students were wearing shorts, beach shoes, and sleeveless shirts to class! I thought everyone was going to a beach party. At the weekend parties my friends wore very casual and very dressy clothes. There were no rules on what to wear and what not to wear. } topic statement } transition words details support

    I listened to everyone's advice and did what I thought was right. I compromised on the clothes I wore because I did not want to be different from everyone else. I learned to budget my time so that I would have plenty for studying and some for having fun with my friends. *Despite my initial frustrations, I found that I could listen to everyone's advice, use my own good judgment, and still be a success.* } conclusion

THESIS STATEMENT   *Should express an opinion*

A good thesis statement serves as a contract between you and the readers, letting your audience know exactly what you are planning to do. It should set the theme for the whole paper, give an indication of the type of paper it will be, and list the ideas you will develop. This statement should contain some key words, usually adjectives that you will use throughout the essay to express your main points. If you follow this step-by-step process, you will be able to write a good composition that will effectively convey your thoughts and hold your readers' attention. Good writing takes practice, and if you are willing to revise and re-create, you will have a much better, finished product. Recognizing your mistakes and correcting them will make you a better writer.

Never use *I* in your thesis statement. Eliminate *you* unless you are writing a persuasion or process essay. In a process paper, you explain to your readers how to do something, and in doing so, you give them commands in a step-by-step process. When writing a persuasion paper, your tone will indicate that it is *your* opinion. If your topic, for example, is "Capital Punishment" and your opening statement is "The death penalty must (not) be abolished," your audience will know that you oppose the death penalty.

The thesis statement and introductory part of any paper are sometimes difficult to write, yet they are the most important parts of the essay. Practice will help you overcome problems.

Avoid the Following Thesis Statements

- I have to write this paper on abortion, but I really don't know anything about it.

- Writing is such a bore, but my teacher made us do this assignment or else I'd fail.   *Two chats*

- I don't know much about this topic, so I'm not sure this is right.

- Oh, I forgot to mention that this is my thesis statement.

- Let me share some ideas on photography with you.

Thesis statement should express an opinion fossés

- I would like to make it perfectly clear to you that I oppose the use of drugs of any kind.

- I hope your dress turns out better than mine; it was a disaster.

Avoid stereotyping, name calling, or berating your audience in any way. Thesis statements like the ones below would discourage your readers from reading further into your essay.

- Any dummy can finish this project. It doesn't take a lot of brains to follow these instructions.

- Anybody who lives in the country certainly isn't very bright.

- Only criminals and crooked politicians can afford to live in luxurious apartments in the big cities.

EXERCISE 38

Look at the following thesis statements and decide whether they

(1) attract the readers' attention
(2) contain a key idea
(3) offend the audience
(4) berate readers
(5) act as stereotypes

Write all the numbers that apply after the sentence.

1. Developing your own black-and-white photographs can be a fascinating and inexpensive hobby. *1, 2*

2. All long-haired teens are into drugs. *3, 5*

3. Everybody who's anybody must see that movie.

4. All college students should study a foreign language before graduating.

5. Our government must cut back on military spending if the country is to survive.

6. People who are on welfare are lazy and unreliable.

7. Misting your ferns will make them greener and healthier.

8. Albuquerque, New Mexico, and Phoenix, Arizona, have many characteristics in common.

9. Blueberry cheesecake is the best dessert in the world.

10. People who ride motorcycles are always in trouble with the law.

Writing Thesis Statements

When you are writing your thesis statement, be aware of the following:

- Make sure that everything that follows agrees with the controlling idea.

- See that everything in the outline meets the established criteria.

- Discuss only one topic and not several.

- Focus on one aspect and not on many.

- Write the thesis statement in the introductory paragraph.

- Relate certain background information.

- Tell your audience what you are going to do and how you plan to do it.

- In process essays, identify items needed to complete the project.

- Use a few key adjectives or adverbs to attract your readers' attention, for example, *economical, easy, enjoyable, quickly, and safely*.

- Tell your audience whether it will be a small, large, fast, lengthy, expensive, or inexpensive project.

- Attract your readers' attention and encourage them to continue reading.

EXERCISE 39

Examine the following thesis statements to see if they are complete (write "OK" or "incomplete"), and decide to which audience you would direct them.

1. Hitchhiking, although economical, can be a very dangerous and an often fatal way to travel.   *OK, young adults*

2. Many people today find that the concept of the "American dream" is only a fairy tale.

3. For a variety of reasons, including peer pressure, many people reject the idea of a monogamous relationship.

4. Traveling country backroads provides peace and quiet, spectacular scenery, and an interesting look at cultural aspects that one does not usually find on the main highways.

5. Spending billions of dollars on space exploration is a waste of taxpayers' hard-earned money.

6. All newspapers contain interesting stories.

7. Everybody needs to invest in insurance.

8. Francesca should get a new wardrobe.

9. Television has become one of the world's greatest sources of economical entertainment.

10. Single people should not be allowed to adopt children.

11. Environmental protection must be closely monitored, or else our planet will be in grave danger in a couple of years.

12. There is a great deal of student cheating that takes place on campus on mid-term and final exams.

13. Dr. Reichen does not care about the progress of his students. He is more interested in researching than in teaching.

14. Marriage should last a lifetime; and couples should think about whether they can make a long-term commitment before they take the final step.

15. If our government does not curb military spending soon, taxpayers will have a tremendous financial burden to bear.

16. One coat of paint on the house will not be enough to restore the walls to their original beauty.

17. Job hunting can be a long, time-consuming, and difficult task.

18. No one likes to deal with quitters.

19. Saving money from a part-time job is one of the greatest problems students face.

20. Attractive floral arrangements can brighten up even the darkest corner of the room.

EXERCISE 40

Look at the following topics and decide what type of essay (narrative, description, comparison/contrast, process, persuasion, reaction) you would write.

1. Gun Control

2. Gambling (lottery, casinos, and so on)

3. Learning to Crochet

4. Dressmaking

5. Guide Dogs

6. Becoming Physically Fit

7. Learning to Prepare Ethnic Foods

8. Leisure Activities

9. Friendship

10. Dating in the 21st Century

11. Two Amusement Parks

12. An Unforgettable Event

WRITING EXERCISE

From the topics listed above, select three topics and write a thesis statement for each one.

Examples:

1. *To avoid the senseless killing of human beings, the government must control the sale and use of guns in this country.*

2. *Gambling either in the lottery or in the casinos would bring in more money into the city for education and welfare programs and provide more jobs for the unemployed.*

INTRODUCTORY PARAGRAPHS

The introductory paragraph is probably the hardest one to write because it sets forth the plan for your essay and must be interesting enough (from the first sentence) to catch the readers' attention and make them want to continue to read what you have written. In writing it, start from the general and work toward the specific. It is best to start any writing with a tentative thesis statement. However, because the introductory paragraph is so difficult to write, you might want to write it after the body of the essay has been completed.

Look at each of the following topics to see how difficult or easy it would be to develop.

Chocolate chip cookies are the best dessert in the whole world. (too narrow)

Even a novice seamstress can make lovely creations by following these simple steps. (good start)

The government must monitor nuclear power plants more carefully to avoid a national disaster. (good start, shows an opinion)

TOPIC SENTENCES

Thesis statements and topic sentences are not the same. Not every paragraph of an essay contains a topic sentence. However, every essay, short or long, must contain a thesis statement. The thesis statement (a sentence, or a paragraph in longer papers) presents the controlling idea of the whole essay. The choice of words you use in it will indicate the type of paper you will be writing. A topic sentence, on the other hand, is like one of the subheadings in your outline. It allows the audience to focus on one part of the whole in a particular paragraph. Many writers begin each paragraph with a topic sentence. In this way, each paragraph forces the reader to think inductively, beginning with a general statement (the topic sentence) that is made clearer by the more specific, supporting details that follow.

Until you start writing longer essays, your concern now will be with the topic sentence. Note that a topic sentence is less general than a thesis statement. The thesis statement includes all of the ideas mentioned in the topic sentences. Let's use the topic of divorce. The thesis statement is *"Immaturity, age, and lack of responsibility are the most common causes for this ever-increasing problem."* The topic sentences are these:

- One of the most common causes is the immaturity on the part of one or both parties.

- Teenage marriages are another factor leading to the extremely high divorce rate.

- In the majority of cases, husband and wife are unable to accept the responsibilities of marriage.

Each of the topic sentences above presents the main idea for each paragraph, and the writer would have to provide details to support that idea.

EXERCISE 41

Read the following details and write a topic sentence that will include all of the information contained below.

Last week when I went through final registration, I found out that the computer had assigned me to the wrong classes. The next day the telephone company sent me a notice that if I did not pay my bill in 48 hours, they would disconnect my service. I had sent a check 15 days prior to the notice. The scanner at the grocery store charged me $1.29 for a 79-cent package of margarine.

_____

_____

_____

Joseph Anderson has taken several courses in creative writing. He has received A's in all of them. Last week the local newspaper published *one of* his articles. Another publisher is interested in a play that he wrote.

_____

_____

_____

My friend Leslie James is studying medicine at the university. Last week she had an anatomy exam and failed it. The other day in class, the students were drawing blood from each other. Leslie fainted in class when she saw her own blood. While observing an autopsy, she became sick to her stomach.

_____

_____

_____

EXERCISE 42

Read the following topic sentences and provide at least five supporting details for each.

Many television shows today portray a great deal of unnecessary violence.

1. *The number of violent acts in a one-hour show has increased.*

2. _____

3. _____

4. _____

5. _____

Because of the need for both parents to work, many families find that their closely knit unit is falling apart as members are moving in opposite directions.

1. ***Children's emotional needs are not met.***

2. _____

3. _____

4. _____

5. _____

The president's new plan for education caused great concern among teachers and students.

1. ***The plan calls for increase in salaries as well as in class size.***

2. _____

3. _____

4. _____

5. _____

Freezing conditions created many problems for travelers during the holiday season.

1. ***De-icing planes causes considerable delays in takeoff and landing.***

2. _____

3. _____

4. _____

5. _____

Our instructor should consider abolishing final exams.

1. ***Students who did not do well all semester won't improve on their final exams.***

2. _____

3. _____

4. _____

5. _____

BODY (SUPPORTING DETAILS)

In this part of the essay, you provide all the details that will support the thesis statement previously made. If you listed some keywords in your thesis statement, what you write in the body will restate and support these and bring coherence into the essay. Keep the following points in mind:

- Include all the details that support the thesis statement.

- Be very specific, or else they will weaken your paper.

- Provide step-by-step specific directions, or else the process you are describing will *not* turn out well.

- Build your ideas from the smallest to the biggest, from the weakest to the strongest, and from the general to the specific.

- Keep looking back at the topic to be sure that the ideas are not wandering off in another direction.

- Brainstorm and re-group your thoughts.

- Make an impact on your readers.

- Support your ideas with statistics from reliable sources.

- Indicate your source of information, either including it in a footnote at the bottom or incorporating it into the body.

- Hint: Write your thesis statement on a sticky note, and put it in a prominent place so you can easily see it and refer back to it as you are writing.

In an essay describing the types of people who attend concerts, you might want to discuss the unwilling spouse who accompanies his wife simply to keep peace in the family. This is how your topic might appear on the exam.

Think of a group activity you have attended recently. What types of people were present? Describe them.

GENERAL	The unwilling husband is rather obvious in his plight.
DETAIL	He tags along behind his wife as she moves past a number of people in her attempt to sit next to a friend who enjoys the same type of music.
DETAIL	The husband's expression is one of fright and boredom.
DETAIL	The former is brought about as he surveys the audience, a sea of unknowns who apparently do not share his interests.
DETAIL	He begins to fret when he realizes that because he does not have an aisle seat, a hasty exit will not be possible without his calling attention to himself.
DETAIL	As the concert begins, he makes snide remarks about the conductor, who reminds him of a chicken "flapping its wings."
DETAIL	He soon falls asleep and begins to snore, distracting those around him.

The details given here support the classification "unwilling spouse." Anyone who has ever attended a concert can identify this person in an instant. Indicate the five characteristics mentioned here about the "unwilling spouse."

Which of the following topic sentences would be the best for a paragraph promoting your friend as a candidate for office? Which is all-inclusive of the characteristics you wish to discuss?

Constantine Kandarakis is the best candidate for class president because he cares about everyone.

Constantine Kandarakis is a great guy and should be class president.

Constantine Kandarakis would make a great president.

The first is the most effective because it emphasizes how the candidate cares about everyone. The other two are too general and do not provide any key words that the writer can develop throughout the paragraph.

If you are watching a political campaign or promoting a friend of yours for a school office, your topic sentence and supporting details might look like this:

Constantine Kandarakis is the best candidate for class president because he cares about everyone. As class president in his junior and senior years in high school, he created a unified student body. His activities promoted more school spirit than was evident in years past. He is well known on our campus as a peer tutor. Last summer he unselfishly gave of himself to work in a summer camp for handicapped children. Constantine is interested in the welfare of all of us, not just in the rich, famous, and powerful. We need someone like Constantine Kandarakis to look out for our interests.

The writer supplied four good reasons why the candidate should be elected based on his background of caring. He probably did not present any new information to the group; he just emphasized what the members already knew. The writer also developed his idea by placing his strongest argument last. This type of writing moves from the general to the specific and is another example of the inductive reasoning approach.

Look at the following outline to see how one writer supplied the details necessary to develop a paragraph on spring.

Thesis Statement: Spring is the most exciting season of the year because it brings colorful relief from the dull, dreary, and monotonous winter.

I. Main Heading 1

    A. Subheading 1

    B. Subheading 2

    C. Subheading 3

    D. Subheading 4

II. Main Heading 2

    A. Subheading 1

    B. Subheading 2

    C. Subheading 3

I. Everything seems to come to life.

    A. Days are longer.

    B. The sun shines brighter.

    C. There is an explosion of color.

    D. Melodious sounds are in the air.

II. This is a period of greater activity.

    A. People plant gardens.

    B. They fix their houses.

    C. Many participate in sports.

Conclusion: The period of rebirth and the brilliant array of colors make spring the most fascinating time of the year.

> ## Spring
>
> Some parts of the country enjoy four distinct seasons. Spring is the most exciting because it brings a colorful relief from the dull, dreary, and monotonous winter. Everything seems to come to life as April and May days become longer and the sun shines warmer and more brightly. There is an explosion of color as the grass turns green; the azaleas burst forth in white, coral, lavender, and pink. The strong, distinct odor of lilacs, wisteria, and honeysuckle fills the air. Dainty, colorful wildflowers dot the countryside, changing it from a desolate brown to a rainbow of colors. The melodious sounds of the returning birds fill the air as they build their nests and await the birth of their offspring. The lazy winter changes to a period of greater activity as more people venture outdoors to plant their gardens, fix up the house, and participate in sports. The period of rebirth and the brilliant array of colors make spring the most fascinating time of the year.

Notice the added information in the revised outline below. Compare it with the earlier version.

Thesis Statement: Spring is the most exciting season of the year. It is a joyous period of rebirth.

I. Main Heading 1	I. Rainbow of colors
A. Subheading 1	A. Flowers in bloom
1. Supporting Detail	1. Yellow daffodils and crocuses
2. Supporting Detail	2. Pink roses, dogwoods, and carnations
3. Supporting Detail	3. White lilies and daisies
4. Supporting Detail	4. Red, fuchsia, and coral azaleas
B. Subheading 2	B. Bright clothing
1. Supporting Detail	1. Pastel, lightweight
2. Supporting Detail	2. Accessories
II. Main Heading 2	II. Scents of the season
A. Subheading 1	A. Perfume of the flowers
1. Supporting Detail	1. Wisteria and honeysuckle
2. Supporting Detail	2. Roses and lilacs
B. Subheading 2	B. Freshly cut grass
C. Subheading 3	C. Tantalizing barbecues

Conclusion: How wonderful are the joys of spring, with its rebirth, perfumed air, tantalizing aromas, and brightly colored clothes!

Notice how the following paragraph becomes more vivid when you add more details. Underline all the details not found in the outline, and then look at how much more interesting the paragraph is.

Spring (revised)

Spring is the most exciting season of the year. It is a joyous period of rebirth. The world bursts into a rainbow of colors and a variety of savory aromas. Flowers bloom and display a brilliant array of hues. Yellow daffodils and crocuses appear everywhere. Pink roses, dogwoods, and carnations grace many gardens. An abundance of white lilies and daisies crowd the new growth in the meadows. Red, fuchsia, and coral azaleas decorate people's front yards. People change their dull dark winter clothes for brighter, happier ones. Women wear pastel-colored, lightweight dresses, skirts, and sweaters. Men sport lighter-colored ties, slacks, and shoes. The wonderful scents of the season fill the air and create a greater awareness of things coming to life. Flowers emit a lovely fragrance as they announce their arrival. The smell of wisteria and honeysuckle overtakes passersby. A more subtle hint of roses and lilacs makes people stop and inhale their pleasant perfume. The unmistakable smell of freshly cut grass reminds all of Mother Earth's rebirth. People leave behind their winter laziness and drag out the barbecue grill. A tantalizing aroma of meat, sauces, and spices once more announces that a new season is here. How wonderful are the joys of spring, with its rebirth, perfumed air, tantalizing aromas, and brightly colored clothes!

The best writing contains many supporting details that enable writers to prove their thesis. All of these details also provide the development necessary for the audience to want to read until the very end.

EXERCISE 43

Look at the following essay on Halloween and answer the following questions:

1. Read the thesis statement at the end of the first paragraph. What do you think the author will discuss?

2. Read the first sentence in paragraph two. This is the topic sentence. What is the key idea that is the basis for this paragraph?

3. Read the paragraph and count the supporting details. Do all of these details relate to the topic sentence?

4. Do the supporting details relate to the thesis statement in the introductory paragraph?

5. Read the conclusion in the last two sentences. Does it summarize the whole essay?

6. Does the conclusion relate to the thesis statement and to the topic sentences?

7. Does the conclusion show readers that this is the end of the essay and that the writer has nothing more to say?

Halloween

Halloween, October 31, is a very important day in the lives of American children. The name is Christian in origin, but today's celebration is somewhat pagan. *The celebration of Halloween changed greatly throughout the centuries as it moved from countries of Celtic influence to the United States.*

The religious significance of this event has changed over the centuries. In the fifth century B.C., October 31st marked the official end of summer and the beginning of the new year in Ireland. It was a time to celebrate the harvest. The Celts believed that in the coming year, the spirits having no bodies would return, looking for warm bodies to possess. Villagers extinguished the fires in their homes so that the spirits would feel unwelcome and move on. The living would then dress in crazy costumes of ghouls and devils and be destructive as they roamed through the village, making lots of noise to scare away the spirits. In later years, some of the children would go from door to door, asking for alms, and distribute whatever they had received to those less fortunate than they. Many centuries later, in an effort to get away from these pagan rituals, the Catholic Church changed the day to commemorate the sacred night before the celebration of All Saints' Day, when the Catholic Church remembers the holy dead, especially martyrs. This night was called "hallowed eve"—now called Halloween. Catholics held special vigils in the cemeteries and offered prayers for the dead.

Today in the United States, the custom has taken on more of a pagan and potentially harmful form of celebration. Children wear costumes and masks resembling people who have died. Sometimes their attire represents people of bad reputation rather than the holy dead of the past. It is common to see children dressed as devils, pirates, Frankenstein, and other evil characters. Children go from house to house, saying, "Trick or treat." They expect to receive candy, fruit, or cookies. Unlike the good children of the past who gave the food to the poor, the children of today will take the treats they collected home and eat them.

The joyous celebration of the past is today often one that can be harmful or even deadly. Children eat too many foods that they collect and become ill. Recently, some mentally deranged people have "celebrated" Halloween by placing razor blades, pins, or poison in the treats that they distribute. Sometimes street gangs inflict pain on innocent people or vandalize buildings and cars.

Halloween has changed greatly over the centuries. From a happy religious celebration, it has become a pagan custom and, for some, one of great fear as innocent people get hurt.

VOCABULARY EXPANSION

Celtic – relating to a group of people who lived in Scotland, Ireland, and Wales

martyrs – people who died for a religious or political cause

vandalize – to intentionally damage something

alms – donations of money or other useful items for the poor

mentally deranged – disturbed, insane

pagan – someone who has no religious beliefs

WRITING EXERCISE

Brainstorm the idea of divorce and provide at least three supporting details to complete the two paragraphs below. Then reread the whole essay to see if the conclusion summarizes everything from the preceding paragraphs.

Divorce

Many couples throughout the world today are seeking divorces. Few people celebrate their 25th anniversary, and even fewer reach the 40th and 50th. Many countries in the past have traditionally opposed divorce. Now, at an alarmingly high rate, divorce is becoming an acceptable practice. *Immaturity, teenage marriages, and lack of responsibility are the most common causes for this ever-increasing problem.*

One of the most common causes is the immaturity on the part of one or both parties. They are unable to communicate their concerns. They shut each other out or else seek solace in others. After a while both spouses find that they no longer share common interests. They prefer to continue to have fun with their former group of unmarried friends.

Teenage marriages are another factor leading to the extremely high divorce rates.

_____supporting detail 1

_____supporting detail 2

_____supporting detail 3

In the majority of cases, husband and wife are unable to accept the responsibilities of marriage.

_____supporting detail 1

_____supporting detail 2

_____supporting detail 3

The threads that formerly held families together are rapidly disintegrating today. Divorce rates are higher throughout the world. Most are caused by unhappy teenage marriages, inability to cope with marital problems, and immaturity.

VOCABULARY EXPANSION

solace – a source of relief from pain

cope – to manage, deal with

disintegrating – falling apart

WRITING EXERCISE

Select one of the topics that you and your classmates brainstormed together. Discuss the ideas, and, working together as a group, write one well-developed essay, using these ideas. Be prepared to write your essay in class.

CONCLUSION

The conclusion, the last part of the essay, informs readers that you have finished telling what you had planned to let them know. You need a smooth ending, not one that leaves your audience awaiting something more. The conclusion of an essay is not like many of today's movies, which leave the door open for a number of sequels. The purpose of the conclusion is to tie everything together and to show that the writer has accomplished what he/she set out to do. For example, in process essays the writer plans to create or change something and, in the end, should have a finished or changed product that turns out well because he/she followed a set of step-by-step instructions. Once again, you mention your strongest points last. Do not present any new information at the end of your paper.

Before deciding that you have finished a writing assignment, review the previously mentioned guidelines to be sure that you have done everything to make your essay a good one.

Make sure that you end on a positive note. In a process essay, encourage readers that the process is *easy, economical, rewarding,* or whatever key adjective you used in the thesis statement. Abrupt endings are frustrating, as readers search for more information or have a number of unanswered questions. The following are *unacceptable in formal writing. Do not incorporate them into your writing.*

- I've run out of ideas, so this must be the end.

- I guess this assignment wasn't so difficult after all.

- I hope your project turned out better than mine. I guess I did something wrong back in step 2.

- So you see that any dummy can make one of these and have it turn out well.

- That's it. You're finished! (This is also poor grammar.)

- Maybe you will have better luck next time.

- If you're smart, you will take my advice and do what I say.

- Nothing to it! A piece of cake!

Make the conclusion short and to the point. The following statements provide a smooth conclusion, persuading readers, or encouraging readers to follow the process you have laid out. They reassure readers that they, too, can create something worthwhile.

- Once you have dried your prints, you can arrange them in a photo album and proudly show them off to your friends.

- Press your new garment, wear it to the next social function you attend, and be the center of attention as everyone compliments you on your skill and cleverness.

Conclusions to narrative and description essays must show an end to the action. Some writers purposely leave their works unfinished so that readers can create their own endings or endure an agonizing wait until the sequel appears. Such endings frustrate rather than appease the audience. Whether it is a happy or sad ending, write it so that the audience expects no more action.

Here is an example of a conclusion for a narrative essay:

As time passed, Mandy learned to accept her loss and slowly began to put together the pieces of her life. She refused to let the world control her. The horrible nightmare was finally over as the plane landed safely amid the shouts of joy from the large crowd who had gathered at the airport.

Consider the following when you write the conclusion:

- Did I give the reader all the information that I had planned to provide?

- Have I said everything that needed to be said?

- Was I strong enough in my thesis statement so that the reader knew my point of view?

- Were my ideas clearly presented?

- Did I provide many supporting details?

- Is the conclusion smooth and complete?

If you answer yes to all of these questions, then you can feel confident that you have done a good job on your paper.

Here are some conclusions that writers need to avoid:

- I hope you agree with me now about legalizing marijuana.

- You probably think I'm crazy, but that's how I feel about the issue.

- That's all I have to say on how to prepare lasagna.

- I guess there's nothing more to say about this topic.

- Gee, I can't think of anything else. It must be all over.

- Well, I managed to struggle through this process. You can do it, too. Have fun!

A conclusion restates the introduction sentence and wraps up what you set out to do. If you were not able to convince the readers with the supporting details, the conclusion won't convince them either.

Be positive and make your readers feel that they, too, can create something great, a joy to behold. Here are some more positive endings that reassure the readers that they, too, can follow the step-by-step procedures and have something to display proudly.

For a process paper on dressmaking:

After giving your garment a final pressing, you will find that you have a lovely dress, one that will get many nice compliments. You have learned an enjoyable activity that will save you a great deal of money in the future.

In persuasion papers, sum up your argument and reinforce your point of view. Look at this persuasion summary:

If the American government does not enforce the 55 mph speed limit on our highways, there will be a further increase in highway fatalities, greater consumption of gasoline, and needless accidents. Life is too precious to waste in this manner.

Conclusions for comparison and contrast papers emphasize the writer's point of view and show that an obvious difference or similarity exists and that the writer's choice is the one that the reader should make in the end also.

After comparing and contrasting living in apartments and houses, you can see that the latter has more advantages. There is greater privacy, more freedom to decorate, and a larger area for storing your belongings and entertaining your friends. Owning a house allows you to be your own boss and gives you the independence you want.

WRITING EXERCISE

Most people found that the energy crisis had many unpleasant effects on them and would be surprised that there actually were any benefits. Do you think the benefits mentioned in the essay below were actually benefits? Can you name any others? What happens to people in times of crisis? Read the following essay, focusing on the details and the thesis statement. Then write a conclusion based on the information provided.

Benefits of the Energy Crisis

A short time ago most of the world was suffering from the ill effects of the energy crisis. Lifestyles were suddenly altered, many rather dramatically. Gasoline was rationed and people had to wait in long lines at the gas station. In some parts of the United States drivers could buy gas only on certain days, depending on the last number or letters of their license plates. Temperatures were regulated in public buildings and new homes became electric, a much more expensive way of heating and cooking.

Despite all the negative aspects of the energy crisis, there were many positive ones as well. When gasoline was at a premium, many drivers could not or would not pay the increase and decided to walk or ride bikes instead. This new trend helped to create healthier Americans who were breathing fresher air due to less pollution and getting more exercise. Those who found it difficult to walk or ride a bicycle formed carpools and helped cut down on pollution.

Advertising campaigns on television and radio and in the newspapers created a greater awareness of what the future would be like if the supplies were depleted. Many found that they could wear an extra sweater, cut down on heating, and save money. When they realized how much they were saving, many people made a more conscious effort to save energy. In 1973, Americans looked seriously at building the Alaskan pipeline, which would supply this country with its own natural resources. This construction project created many jobs for unemployed Americans. It also helped to prove to the world that America would not be dominated by the oil-producing countries.

_____

_____

_____

_____

_____

_____

One possible conclusion would be the following. See what other conclusions you can create.

Although many people focused on the negative aspects of the energy crisis, there were several positive outcomes. People exercised more, saved money on energy, and looked for ways to make the country more self-sufficient.

Advanced Writing

ESL

CHAPTER 5

Writing Techniques

Chapter 5
Writing techniques

TRANSITIONS

Transitions are words that help ideas and words flow smoothly as the reader moves from sentence to sentence, paragraph to paragraph, or idea to idea. Such words enable the reader to follow the sequence of events in the narrative, and they are very important for bringing coherence into your essay. In explaining a process, the writer must show the proper sequence of tasks if the final product is to turn out well. When you want to contrast and compare, you need a special set of transition words to show your audience how to distinguish one set from the other. You need transition words also to introduce examples to prove your point and lend support to your argument. Smooth transitions are important for expressing yourself clearly in your writing. If you fail to connect your ideas properly, it will seem as if the information in your essays was there just to fill up space.

The words and expressions listed below are not the only ones that you can use to make smooth transitions, but they are the most common.

TRANSITIONAL DEVICES

Purpose	Transitional Words
1. TO ADD (Process and Narrative)	also, and, and then, too, plus, in addition, furthermore, moreover, another, first, second, likewise, equally important, again, similarly, besides, especially, not only ... but also
2. TO PUT IN TIME ORDER (Process and Narrative)	now, then, before, after, afterward, earlier, later, immediately, soon, next, in a few days, meanwhile, gradually, suddenly, finally, previously, today, tomorrow, as soon as, until, when, at last, after that, at the time, once, while, farther, in a little while
3. TO PUT IN SPACE ORDER (Description)	near, far, far from, in front of, beside, along, in the rear of, beyond, above, below, to the right (left), around, surrounding, on one side, inside, outside, alongside, in the distance, foreground, background, across, closer, farther, here, there, against
4. TO COMPARE	in the same way, similarly, just like, just as, likewise, in a like manner, by comparison
5. TO CONTRAST	but, still, however, on the other hand, on the contrary, yet, nevertheless, despite, in spite of, even though, in contrast, conversely, although, granted that, not
6. TO SHOW CAUSE AND EFFECT	because, since, so, consequently, as a result, therefore, then, accordingly, hence, thus, it follows that
7. TO SHOW PURPOSE	for this reason, for this purpose, so that, so that this may happen
8. TO EMPHASIZE (Persuasion)	indeed, in fact, surely, necessarily, certainly, without any doubt, in any event, truly, again, to repeat
9. TO GIVE EXAMPLES	for example, for instance, as an illustration, specifically, to be specific, as proof, that is, such as, thus, to illustrate
10. TO SUMMARIZE	in summary, in conclusion, as has been stated, in brief, to sum up, in short, thus, finally

Transitional Adverbs

A certain group of adverbs are used for creating smooth transitions (flow) between two main clauses or other ideas represented in a sentence. Their purpose is to introduce additional information, show steps in a process, or present a contrast. They may occur at the beginning or middle of a sentence. Some may be interchangeable, and others may not. Look at how to use them in a sentence. Here is a list of transitional adverbs:

accordingly	instead	so
also	meanwhile	therefore
besides	moreover	then
consequently	nevertheless	thus
finally	next	
furthermore	otherwise	
however	rather than	
indeed	similarly	

At the beginning of a sentence:

TRANSITIONAL ADVERB, + SUBJECT + VERB
(main clause)

Phil is a highly intelligent person. **However,** he is too lazy for this job.

The horses are getting ready for the race. **Meanwhile,** the jockeys are listening to the trainers.

Or they may join two main clauses.

S + V + ; TRANSITIONAL ADVERB, + S + V
(main clause)   (main clause)

Jeff won a scholarship to a state university; **nevertheless,** he prefers to stay in town to complete his studies.

You need to remove the pins first; **otherwise,** you will break the needle as you stitch over them.

They may also come in the middle of a sentence between two elements of the main clause.

SUBJECT, + TRANSITIONAL ADVERB, + VERB

Alfred, **rather than** his brothers, is taking over the company.

The government, **moreover,** wants to raise taxes to pay for the new project.

Other Transition Words

Yet is used with questions and negative answers and indicates a time up to the present. It usually comes at the end of the sentence and is used mostly with the present perfect tense.

The movie hasn't begun **yet**.

Have you read that book **yet**?

Yet can also be a coordinating conjunction used to show contrast similar to *but.* Notice that a comma separates the two independent clauses.

Monica does not have much money, **yet** she has a new car.

That man is the richest in the world, **yet** he is not happy.

Still indicates a continuing action in progress at a given time in the past, present, or future. Still follows the conjugated verb *to be* and precedes other verbs except auxiliaries in questions.

Ming is **still** studying physics at the university.

Toshi **still** rode his bicycle to work after he had graduated.

Will Mohammad **still** be teaching this class next year?

Still can also be used as a conjunctive adverb meaning *but*. With this construction, *still* will be followed by an independent clause.

Tara's father is very busy; **still** he has time to have fun with his family.

Tony has not won the lottery; **still** he keeps trying.

So that and *in order to* both indicate purpose, but their grammatical structures are different.

SO THAT + S + V (CONJUGATED)

IN ORDER TO + SIMPLE FORM OF VERB

The students practiced every day **so that they could improve** their skills.

The students practiced every day **in order to improve** their skills.

But and *however/nevertheless* show contrast, but their structures and punctuation are different. Good writers do not begin a sentence with *but*, but they can use *however/nevertheless*. When using *but* as a conjunction with two main clauses, always use a comma (,) before the word *but*. When using *however/nevertheless* with two main clauses, use a semicolon (;) before and a comma (,) after the conjunction.

I don't have the money now, **but** I will have it at 6:00.

He bought a parking decal, **but** that did not guarantee a parking space.

Toshiko is having problems; **nevertheless**, she keeps on writing.

The Garcias had not found a house to buy; **however**, this did not keep them from looking every weekend.

But rather also shows contrast, and it is used with nouns, pronouns, adjectives, and adverbs. Notice that the main clause in each of these is negative and that there is a comma (,) before the conjunction.

NOUN:	He doesn't need money, **but rather** love, since he is already a millionaire.
PRONOUN:	I don't want the blue one, **but rather** the red one.
ADJECTIVE:	Don't paint the house red, **but rather** yellow, since all the others are light colored.
ADVERB:	They did not drive slowly to the hospital, **but rather** quickly, as the mother was about to deliver her baby.

Notice the punctuation and the meaning conveyed in the following sentences.

No one knows the artist personally. Rafael, however, is familiar with his works.

It conveys the idea of *but* uses a different punctuation pattern. *However* and *nevertheless* are conjunctive adverbs like *also, furthermore, thus, then,* and *therefore* and are set off with the same punctuation.

Because and *because of* also mean the same but the grammatical structures are different.

BECAUSE + SUBJECT + VERB

BECAUSE OF + NOUN

Because it was raining, we arrived late. (S + V)

Because of the rain, we arrived late. (Noun)

The following pairs are also interchangeable.

also-too   **in addition to-besides**

furthermore-moreover   **likewise-equally-similarly**

alongside-beside

Around and *surrounding* (as prepositions) can usually be interchangeable if they indicate a complete circle enclosing something at any given time.

Phil built a fence *around* (surrounding) his property.

The mountains *surrounding* (around) the village protected it from the wind.

However, you must use *around* when the action indicates that eventually there will be a complete circle.

We walked *around* the house, inspecting the paint job.

The father drove **around** the block several times as the children looked for their missing dog.

Both actions eventually will form complete circles.

Around meaning *almost* (adverb), however, cannot be interchanged with *surrounding*.

It was *around* five o'clock when we arrived home.

He had *around* fifteen dollars in his pocket.

Too and *also* indicate in addition to.

I want some ice cream, and my son does, *too* (also).

The Millers also visited Peru. The Millers visited Peru, *too*.

Furthermore and *moreover* indicate that the speaker/writer is going to add more information to what has already been said. Both usually come at the beginning of a sentence.

Furthermore (moreover), I believe that Steve will be more honest and caring.

Alongside and *beside* show location next to another person or object.

It is prohibited to park *alongside* (beside) a fire hydrant.

Beautiful red roses grew *beside* (alongside) the house.

In addition to and *besides* also indicate that more information is forthcoming.

In addition to (besides) the gray shoes, Melanie bought a scarf and hat.

Harry plans to visit Spain and Portugal *besides* (in addition to) Austria.

Note the difference between *besides* (more information) and *beside* (location).

Two expressions can be similar but actually have different meanings. *In the rear of* indicates the back part of something (car, house, classroom). *Behind* indicates the location of an object farther back from another object.

On cold, rainy days, we leave our umbrellas *in the rear of* the classroom. (inside)

Joe parked his car *behind* the house. (outside of the house)

In the distance (preposition) usually implies something that you can see away from where you are. *Far* (adverb) indicates something at a distance that you cannot see.

We live *far* from the university.

The lights *in the distance* twinkled like bright stars.

Foreground describes an area at the very front of a picture or scene. *In front of* indicates a specific location immediately before a given object. *Background* denotes an area at the very back of a picture or scene. *Behind/in back of* shows location of an object immediately after another object.

In the foreground, Harry is racing down the highway to his house, which is *in front of* the two large trees.

He has set out several pumpkins for Halloween *behind* the trees.

In the *background,* the city is busy with the preparations for the big event.

The following time order transitions can be interchangeable.

meanwhile-at the same time	**now-at this moment**
next-then	**as soon as-when**
lastly-finally (when they show a sequence)	
afterward-later (unless you are comparing *sooner* and *later*)	

There is, however, a distinct difference between *immediately* and *suddenly*. When the event is unexpected, use *suddenly*.

> I went to pay the cashier and **suddenly** I realized that I had no money.
>
> After I realized that my car had been stolen, I **immediately** called the police.

Sometimes pairs of transition words are interchangeable with no grammatical differences. Other times, however, the way they are used in sentences is completely different. As you learn these words, think of them as

- signals that are alerting you to a change in time or space

- showing similarity or difference

- moving chronologically from one step to another

When you are writing a process, you want your audience to see you move from one step to another or from one place to another. The discussion below on how to fry eggs, a very simple process, uses some of the transitional words in the time order category. Notice how the transition is made from one step to the next here. Each of these sentences shows the chronological order of the steps in the process.

Frying Eggs

On weekends when you have more time to eat breakfast, you may want to have something special like fried eggs. Making this part of a delicious meal is easy and takes *less than five minutes. Before* you begin to cook, line up your utensils and ingredients. *This way* you will not waste time running around looking for them *as* you are cooking. *Now* that everything is at hand, turn on the burner to medium high *and* set the lightly greased frying pan on it. Take the eggs *one at a time and* tap them lightly against the inside of the pan. *Then* hold the egg with both hands and gently push your thumbs through the crack. *Next,* separate the egg *and* drop the contents into the pan. Put two or three eggs in *at once,* depending on whether it is a large or small pan. *Immediately* turn down the heat so that the eggs do not burn. *As soon as* the whites start to get golden and the yolks are firm, slide a spatula under them. *As soon as* you remove them from the pan, put them on a plate. *Finally,* add a little salt and pepper to taste. Your tasty fried eggs are ready to eat.

Fallingwater

Fallingwater is one of the greatest architectural masterpieces in domestic design. As tourists travel the wooded walkway along Bear Run stream, they see this magnificent house in the distance. It appears to float above a natural waterfall deep among the trees. The cantilevered terraces rising over thirty feet and hanging over the waterfall sharply contrast with the rugged reinforced concrete and the smooth-flowing water below. Rock ledges and trees are on all sides of the house that served as a weekend retreat for the Kauffman family. Across the stream, multicolored flowers brighten the earthy tones of the house.

On an autumn day the colorful changing leaves surrounding the structure blend with the darker stones of the house. To the left, sandstone columns anchor smaller terraces, allowing the house to expand horizontally. The breathtaking view of Frank Lloyd Wright's plan to unite nature and structure is one that visitors will long remember.

EXERCISE 44

Answer the following questions based on the story "Fallingwater."

1. The writer uses a number of transitions that connect several short sentences to make the ideas flow more smoothly. Which transitions are used?

2. How did the writer present the supporting details? From least to most important? From general to specific? From one location to another?

3. Do the supporting details and the conclusion relate directly to the thesis statement?

Writing out every step in a process is time consuming, but absolutely necessary. If you eliminate one or more steps, the process will not turn out successfully.

Note the transition words in the following process essay and see how they differ from ones in the previous writing.

EXERCISE 45

Read the story "The Pisaq Ruins" to see how the author uses transition words to move smoothly from one idea to the next. Underline all the transition words.

The Pisaq Ruins

The first day of our vacation in Peru last summer was action packed. The alarm rang at 6:30, <u>and suddenly</u> we were up and ready for the day's activities. <u>Before</u> we got dressed, we ordered breakfast in our room to save ourselves some time. As soon as we had finished eating, we ran downstairs to catch our tour bus. Immediately after we boarded, the driver set out for the Pisaq ruins. Soon after leaving Cuzco, we came upon the magnificent ruins of Sacsayhuaman, a former Inca fortress. In a few moments we were on the ground, exploring and photographing the majestic walls that jut in and out, resembling the teeth of a jaguar. Afterward, we climbed to one of the small peaks and saw a breathtaking view of the valley below. After that we continued on a bumpy road through the mountains to our destination. Suddenly, a herd of llamas darted in front of the bus, forcing us to stop rather abruptly. It was worth it to get a picture of them in their natural habitat, but the sudden stop certainly jarred our nerves.

When we had finally arrived at the ruins, we found that we had to park the bus and continue our climb on foot. Our guide had previously said that the distance would be a couple of kilometers; on the contrary, we had to walk about six kilometers. Gradually, we made the climb of about 1,000 feet. However, for those of us unaccustomed to the 13,000-foot altitude, it was difficult to breathe. At last, we found ourselves at the top, overlooking the terrace farms that had once served as the food supply of hundreds of varieties of corn and potatoes for the Incas.

The return trip was less eventful, and in a short time, we found ourselves back at the hotel. Later we took a short nap and felt rested enough to visit the markets of Cuzco.

Vocabulary Expansion

fortress – a large heavily protected area

Inca – ancient Indian group from South America

jut – project (v)

jaguar – large animal of the cat family—like a leopard, only bigger

bumpy – marked by ups and downs in a rough road

llama – South American animal related to the camel; known for its fine, soft fur

jarred – shook; had a disagreeable effect on

EXERCISE 46

Read the following paragraph and underline the transitional adverbs. Reread it and look at how the adverbs allow the sentences to flow smoothly. Decide whether each adverb 1) adds information, 2) is part of a process, 3) shows contrast, or 4) draws a conclusion.

Wayne is a hardworking student in a premedical program. **Besides** (*adds information*) taking five classes, he holds down a full-time job as a cabinet installer. **Nevertheless** (*contrast*), he completes all of his tasks on time. Rather than spend many hours watching television, he works on his assignments. Consequently, his grades are among the best in the class. Therefore, he feels good about himself. He also exercises in the gym three times per week. Otherwise, he would not be physically fit and would be a poor example for members of his future profession. His roommate, however, is just the opposite. He is also in the same program, so he tries to study as much as Wayne.

Paco, however, has a number of girlfriends and can't concentrate on his school work. Instead, he spends a lot of time in the gym. Then he goes to the pool to cool off and relax. Next, he finds himself surrounded by beautiful women. Finally, he realizes that he has wasted the afternoon. Consequently, his grades are not good. Furthermore, the dean has already warned him that he may be expelled. He is, therefore, under the careful supervision of his instructors. Paco had better study harder; otherwise, there will be one less premedical student in the university. Both have agreed to study together; otherwise, Paco will not pass his exams and become a doctor.

PROOFREADING

The careful process of rereading and correcting mistakes is called proof-reading. It is not limited only to composition writing. Writers should proofread letters, business correspondence, job-related reports, and anything that they write. A well-thought-out essay with many supporting details can receive a low grade if it is cluttered with grammatical and spelling errors. If you spend a great deal of time creating an interesting piece of writing, you will want your readers to be able to read and understand it. You will also not appreciate your instructor's red marks all over your writing. You will tire of reading "Great essay, but your minor errors spoiled it."

If a piece of writing is properly proofread, it creates a better image of the writer. Class assignments, job applications, lab reports, and work reports that are well written and proofed will create a better impression. An employer will not be pleased with a secretary who constantly misspells words or uses incorrect punctuation. The clients who receive these letters will not be impressed either. As a rule, all letters soliciting information get better attention if they are free of errors. Poorly written materials distract and turn off readers very quickly, and if the writers are requesting information, they may not receive it as a result of their carelessness.

Carelessness in proofreading led to a great deal of embarrassment for administrators of a local library in San Jose, California, who thought they would attract more of the non-native groups to use their facilities by putting up a banner saying "Welcome" in twenty-seven languages. The sign was to be an impressive part of the library's rededication ceremony. However, a Filipino security guard realized that the expression in his native language said "circumcision" instead. (In some religious groups, circumcision is performed as a ceremony of purification.) The town's 60,000 Filipinos would have been greatly offended by this mistake. Painters also incorrectly spelled the greeting in several other languages. The library had to destroy the $10,000 banner and the three-month painting job because someone had neglected to proofread it carefully. Don't be embarrassed by something you wrote because you did not have time to correct your mistakes.

Don't be afraid to do a major overhaul on something you have written. Great writers edit and rewrite numerous times before they submit their articles for publication. You will learn from your mistakes and become a better writer as a result.

Your proofreading can begin immediately after you have finished your writing. Reread your paper to see if you can detect any major errors. Try to allow yourself enough time to set the paper aside for a couple of days, and then reread it when your thoughts are not so fresh in your mind. A few days after you have written something, you will be more likely to find your errors. Keep a dictionary or spell checker by your side every time you write something. Never consider spelling errors minor. With electronic spellers and spell checkers in computers today, there is no excuse for not checking your work. When your instructor permits you to use a dictionary for in-class writings, allow yourself enough time at the end of the period to check any words that are problematic. Put some mark under them so that you can find them easily. *Do not waste time looking up every word as you write it.* This practice will cause you to lose valuable time and perhaps miss deadlines. Your focus will be interrupted and you can lose your train of thought.

When you are not in class, read your paper aloud to see how it sounds. Sometimes it is easier to catch mistakes when you hear them rather than when you look at them. Always focus on individual words rather than on the whole sentence. If you allow yourself enough time, you might be able to tape your writing and listen to the replay. This will allow you to determine whether the writing makes sense or not. Concentrate on your errors (punctuation, spelling, run-ons, comma splices, and so on.) Once you are certain that you have eliminated these errors, you can proceed to look for the other problems mentioned in the checklist below. Use a highlighting pen or an ink color different from the original one to indicate your errors. If using a computer, you will have little trouble quickly locating and correcting the mistakes that have been highlighted. Ask someone to help you proof your paper for content, grammar, and spelling. Finally, check the revised copy for overall presentation. One or two minor "repairs" at this point are acceptable, but your instructor is less likely to look favorably on sloppy corrections.

You and your instructor will be satisfied with the extra effort you have put into writing a quality essay.

PROOFREADING CHECKLIST

Use the following checklist to see that your papers are in excellent written form. After your instructor has graded your paragraphs or essays, look at your errors and place a check (✓) in the box corresponding to each mistake.

Active/Passive Voice						
Apostrophe						
Article						
Capitalization						
Colon						
Comma						
Comma Splice						
Conclusion						
Contraction						
Diction (idioms, wrong word)						
Fragment						
Improper Paragraphing						
Lack of Supporting Details						
Parallel Structure						

Period					
Plagiarism					
Preposition					
Pronoun Agreement					
Pronoun Reference					
Quotation					
Redundancy					
Run-On Sentence					
Sentence Sense (unintelligibility)					
Shift					
Mood					
Point of View					
Verb Tense					
Slang					
Spelling					
Subject/Verb Agreement					
Thesis Statement					
Title					
Too Brief					
Topic Sentence					
Underlining					
Verbosity					
Weak Conclusion					
Weak Introduction					
Word Choice					
Word Division					
Word Missing					
Word Order					

EXERCISE 47

On his science essay exam, Abdul had to write about eclipses of the sun. Proofread his answer and make all necessary corrections. Rewrite the whole essay in its corrected form. The essay includes errors in spelling, punctuation, capitalization, articles, word choice, verb tense, and redundancy. Be a super scholar and find all of them. Refer to the Proofreading Checklist for guidance.

Solar Eclipse

A soler eclipse ocurs when the moon passes between the son and the earth, and the three form a strait line. Their is a large shadow on the sun, causing sum areas to be in darkness not all places will see the same amount of the eclipse. the closer an area is to the total eclipse, the less light poeple are able to see. Although the moon appears to cover the sun completely. It is only an ilusion. The moon is one four-hundredth as large as the sun, but the moon is closer to the earth and appeared to block the sun out.

The last total solar eclispe visible in north america took place in the year 2017, some 38 years after it's predecessor. Scientists advice those watching the eclipse to not look directly at the sun. They would not even use sunglasses or filters. To due so could damage the retina of eye and cause irreversible blindness.

EXERCISE 48

Brigit, a Danish student studying in the United States, had a wonderful opportunity to visit part of the American Northwest last summer. She and some friends visited one of the big national parks. For one of her first composition assignments, she chose to write about what she had seen there. Read her paragraph and correct all the errors that Brigit forgot to change when she proofread it. There are *29 errors* in the following areas: spelling, punctuation, capitalization, redundancy, embedded questions, S/V agreement, adjective agreement, wrong words, and pronouns.

Yellowstone National Park

The State of wyoming has many parks, but the most beautiful is Yellowstone National Park. This is the place where millions of acres provides a natural habitat for moose bears elk and deer. They wander freely, grazing on the lush green grass and provide tourist with interesting seens for to fotograph. A friend of our asked me, "what was the most exciting thing did you see there?" I told he about the fascinating geyser, Old Faithful. Their are many geysers, mud holes, and hot springs, but Old faithful is the biggest and more spectacular. I told my friend how people visited there all year long except at the time when the snow was very high during the winter. He did not no that recently there was many forest fires there and that tourist cannot enter to the park. Its to bad that careless smokers destroy the environment that we foreigners should like to enjoy on ours visits.

VOCABULARY EXPANSION

acre – a measure of land equal to 4,840 square yards

forest – a large group of trees

grazing – the way horses and cows eat grass in an open field

lush – abundant

geyser – underground spring that shoots up intermittent spurts of hot water

moose – type of hoofed animal that lives in the forests of northern America and Eurasia

elk – type of large northern deer

deer – hoofed animals, including elk, moose, caribou, and reindeer

REVISING

Plan to spend time revising your work. As you become more proficient in writing, you will need less time for this activity. Whether you are writing an in-class essay or one to be completed out of class, put aside enough time to make revisions, allowing several days for out-of-class assignments. Look at each revision you make as a different writing. You will be able to see things that you did not see the previous day.

If you have access to a computer or a word processor, the revising process can be easy and fun. While it may take you over an hour to rewrite a fairly short essay by hand, you can cut and paste, check spelling, and reword your document in about fifteen to twenty minutes or less on a computer. Remember, however, when using the spell check feature on your computer, that it alerts you to only the incorrectly spelled, non-existent words. If you write the word "there" when you need "their," spell check will not alert you to the mistake. You still need to do the final reading and editing before you decide that your assignment is complete. Always make an extra copy of your work. If your work ever gets lost, you will always have a spare copy to submit.

Many writers, even the best, find it hard to eliminate words, paragraphs, and pages and/or rewrite them. Somehow they feel that the words are part of themselves and do not wish to lose them. However, once they make the changes and overcome this desire not to cut, they can be more objective about creating a better piece of writing. Your final copy often looks very different from the original one. Focus on the following questions to help yourself make a good revision.

Whole Essay:

- Have you written a title for your essay?

- If you underlined the title, you need to erase the underline.

- Does your title fit the assigned topic?

- Is what you have written appropriate for your level of writing?

- Did you narrow your topic, or is it still too broad?

- Did you stick to the topic throughout the essay?

- Did you write a thesis statement in the introductory paragraph?

- Does every idea in your paper relate to the thesis statement?

- Have you addressed your essay to the proper audience?

- Is the tone appropriate?

- Have you used transitions that allow you to move smoothly from one sentence to another, paragraph to paragraph, idea to idea?

- Are there enough supporting details?

- Have you berated or stereotyped any individual or groups?

- Do your statements move from the general to the specific?

- Have you saved your best point for last?

- If this is a process paper, are all the steps chronological?

- Are your ideas clear?

- Have you used the correct method?

- Have you followed your outline?

- Does the conclusion let your audience know that this is really the end of your paper?

Paragraphs:

- Did you provide a topic sentence for each paragraph?

- Do all the details support the topic sentence?

- Do all of these details relate to your thesis statement?

- Is all of the grammar correct?

Sentences:

- Are all of the sentences complete, or are there some fragments?

- Did you check punctuation?

- Are your ideas logical?

- Do your sentences contain any vague antecedents?

- Do all subjects and verbs agree?

- Have you used pronouns correctly?

- Do adjectives modify nouns and pronouns, and do adverbs modify verbs,

  adjectives, and adverbs?

- Is the word order correct?

- Did you begin each sentence with a capital letter?

Words:

- Did you avoid the use of slang?

- Is your writing verbose?

- Have you chosen your words carefully?

- Is your vocabulary appropriate for your audience?

- Is your paper full of clichés, or have you been careful in your word choice?

- Does your paper satisfy the word requirement?

- Does your vocabulary reflect the tone?

- Have you checked your spelling?

- Have you checked the meaning of some words in the dictionary?

The keys words to remember in revising your papers are in this chart.

ADD	...more supporting details
	...transition words to make your ideas flow smoothly
ASK	...for help and exercises from instructors on ways to correct your problem areas
CUT	...eliminate anything that does not pertain to the topic
	...repetitions (redundancy)
	...slang
	...verbosity
CHANGE	...words that you keep repeating; find synonyms to replace them (use a thesaurus)
	...your focus if it is too broad or too narrow
SHIFT	...sentences and paragraphs so that your paper makes sense
	...physically cut and paste to see if the new arrangement sounds better
SHARE	...your paper with friends to see if they understand your ideas

Remember, as displayed in the previous table, the letters <u>AA</u> <u>CC</u> <u>SS</u> are your keys to making good revisions.

As you look back at your title, decide whether it is the most appropriate for your paper. Does it catch your audience's attention? Is it too narrow or too broad? Review your thesis statement. If you find that you have none, create one, and make sure that every sentence that follows relates to it. Indicate your method by your choice of words.

Look at the topic sentence of each paragraph. Make sure that all of the sentences in the paragraph support and expand on the topic sentence. Leave your strongest point for last. If you have not, change the order of your sentences. If you are having problems writing enough details, you need to brainstorm again. As you make changes, focus on your spelling, grammar, and punctuation. As you are writing, do not break your concentration by checking the spelling of every word. Just draw a small wavy line under each word and look up *all* words when you have finished writing the whole paper.

If you are planning to spread the writing over a period of days, check what you have written at the end of each writing session. In this way you will be able to make some of the revisions as you go along.

When you come to the end of the paper, look at the conclusion. If it does not seem to put a final note on your paper, you need to revise it or provide one that does. Review what you have written to see that you have fulfilled the contract that you made with your readers in the thesis statement. If you did not do what you set out to accomplish, you might need to revise your thesis statement, the essay content, or the conclusion.

Look at the following rough draft in which the student provided almost no descriptive words. After noting the lack of adjectives for what was to be a description paper, the student then went back and brainstormed the idea again. Compare this copy with the finished paragraph that follows it to see how the adjectives the student incorporated into the essay made the writing come to life.

Forgotten and Abandoned (Rough Draft)

Across our highways motorists pass numerous barns that are falling apart. This is because no one cares about them. Despite the passage of time, the paths around them show ruts of vehicles that traveled around them. The boards or logs once provided support and storage. Today, they shelter many animals. The rafters are just a pile of junk. Cobwebs make it impossible to see the depth of the barns. Some travelers probably think about memories that surrounded them in the past. An overwhelming gloom makes you want to leave this place, but the trees surrounding the barn seem to engulf you with their long branches.

Forgotten and Abandoned (Final Copy)

Across the modern highways of America, motorists pass numerous dark, lonely, and desolate barns that bear evidence of the ravages of time and weather. Their deterioration, in part, is due to a general lack of attention and care. Despite the passage of time, the paths around them show deep ruts from the tractors and other farm vehicles that, in their heyday, encircled them daily. The weak gray weatherbeaten boards or logs, which long ago provided support and storage, today shelter a multitude of creatures, such as squirrels, birds, and field mice. Many of the rafters, split and hanging loosely by a few rusty nails, now resemble a pile of useless boards. Lacy gray cobwebs make it impossible to see the true dimensions or depth of the structure. An overwhelming sense of gloom pervades these desolate relics of more prosperous eras. As the travelers continue on their way, some will wonder how many memories blew in the strong winds, tamed by the surrounding mighty oaks, and raked into the safe solitude of these barns.

How many adjectives did you find that made the description of the old barns come alive?

Underline the adjectives. If you do not know the meaning of all of them, look them up in the dictionary.

What would this essay be like without these descriptive words?

How did the second description make it easier to visualize these old structures?

CORRECTION MARKS

abbrev.	abbreviation	(;)	semicolon error
adj.	adjective	(:)	colon error
adv.	adverb	(?)	question error
awk.	awkard construction	∧	insert comma
caps.	uppercase, capital letters	∧	insert period
thr‿ough	close up, all one word	˅	insert apostrophe
CS	comma splice	pron. ref.	pronoun reference
dang. part.	dangling participle	red.	redundant
diction	need to revise the way you said it	RO	run-on or fused sentence
frag.	fragment, not complete sentence	shift	shift in person, mood, tense
∧	insert	SS	sentence sense; can't understand
TREE	lowercase letters	tense	wrong verb tens
¶	new paragraph	h/u‿o/s e	transpose letters
no ¶	no new paragraph	verb.	verbose
//	parallel structure	WW	wrong word
pl	plural		

Another student wrote this amusing essay on one of his first experiences with American do-it-yourself activities. Notice the number of errors in the original, the instructor's corrections in the second, and the student's final corrections.

Do-It-Yourself Activities

My life was effected by do-it-yourself activities on diferents aspects because I was accustomed not to do anything. In addition, I could learn how to perform my jobs. As an ilustration, I will speak about my first here. My first trouble was when I used the wash maching; this was the end of the world because I have never washed in my house, already that my mother did that. Do-it-myself is not a easy job.

I said that it was not easy job because I need not only to learn how the wash but also the diferents methods for this activities. With the practice, I learned to by soap and select the clothes. I learned this when during my first time I put a red T-shirt together with a white pant and when it ended the process

all of that was red. Then, I said "Don't put more colored clothes together with white clothes." Learning to do-it-myself was hard, but it teached me that it was the job to learn by myself because my maching won't do it for me.

Gradually, I learn other thing. Learning to perfect such jobs depends of diferents aspects such as the money, the practice, and the time. Because if you see the result of your activities, you can look for not only the satisfaction, but also its perform by yourself. I think, the situation makes that you learned and that if at the start one problem effected your life, right now that is not a problem for you.

Do-It-Yourself Activities

sp.   *sing.ww*
My life was effected by do-it-yourself activities on diferents aspects because I

diction
was accustomed not to do anything. In addition, I could learn how to perform my jobs.

sp.   *don't say it; do it!*   *ww*
As an ilustration, I will speak about my first here. My first trouble was when I used the

sp.
wash maching; this was the end of the world because I have never washed in my house,

diction   *To*   *sp.*   *tense agr.*
already that my mother did that. Do-it-myself is not a easy job.

sp.   *diction*
I said that it was not easy job because I need not only to learn how the wash but

adj/noun   *sing.*
agr.   also the diferents methods for this activities. With the practice, I learned to by soap and
ww   *sp.*
select the clothes. I learned this when during my first time I put a red T-shirt together

pl.   *awk.*
with a white pant and when it ended the process

vague
all of that was red. Then, I said "Don't put more colored clothes together with white

irreg. verb
clothes." Learning to do-it-myself was hard, but it teached me that it was the job to learn

sp.   *ww*
by myself because my maching won't do it for me. *tense agr.*

tense   *pl.*   *ww* *sing.*
Gradually, I learn other thing. Learning to perfect such jobs depends of diferents

ww
aspects such as the money, the practice, and the time. Because if you see the result of

ww   *awk.*
your activities, you can look for not only the satisfaction, but also its perform by yourself.

tense
I think the situation makes that you learned and that if at the start one problem effected

sp.
your life, right now that is not a problem for you.

diction

After making the suggested corrections, the student revised his essay to look like this.

Do-It-Yourself Activities

Because I am not accustomed to doing anything for myself, my life has been affected by "do-it-yourself" activities on different occasions. I have had to learn how to perform many jobs. My first experience occurred when I used the washing machine. This seemed like the end of the world because my mother always did the washing at our house. Do-it-yourself was my first class, and immediately I learned that "do-it-myself" was not an easy job.

I said that it was not easy because I needed to learn how to wash, using different methods. With practice I learned to buy soap and sort out the clothes. I learned this the first time I put a red T-shirt together with a pair of white pants. When I had finished washing, everything was red. Then I said to myself, "Don't put any more colored clothes together with white clothes." Learning to do it myself was hard, but it taught me that I needed to wash my own clothes because the machine would not do the work for me.

Gradually I learned many things through practice and time. When I saw the result of these activities, I was able to take satisfaction in performing them myself. Experience made me learn that if at first a problem affected my life, I would change the result and no longer have any problems.

Advanced Writing

ESL

CHAPTER 6

Essay Types

Chapter 6
Essay types

WRITING ESSAYS

When you take standardized or in-class essay exams, you will have a certain time limit to write a well-developed composition consisting of approximately 250 to 300 words. The topic that is selected for you should be one to which all adult students will be able to relate. You must write on that topic only. Writing on another topic will result in no credit, and you will have to repeat the exam at a later date.

The following helpful hints will assist you in understanding and mastering this part of an exam.

- Practice writing the essay topics provided at the end of this text.

- Work under timed conditions so that you can gauge the amount of time you will need to finish your essay.

- Write on at least eight of the topics in this book so that you will have a good idea of how long it takes to write.

- Familiarize yourself with the format for each essay type.

- Read the words carefully, and make sure that you understand the topic *before* you begin to write.

- Organize your time so that you can complete the assignment in the allotted time and feel good about what you have written.

- Take a few minutes to think about the topic first.

- Brainstorm to get some ideas about the topic. This allows you to get ideas down on paper. Then you can rearrange and eliminate any that are not related.

- Cluster or group all your ideas so that writing will come more easily and logically.

- Outline the brainstorming. It will help set up the plan for writing the essay.

- Create a good thesis statement that will control the whole essay.

- Begin to develop your essay, one step at a time.

- Keep looking back as you write on the topic and thesis statement, so that the essay does not lose focus.

- Allow about ten minutes at the end to proof and revise.

- Check for spelling, subject/verb agreement, sentence structure, and development.

- Think of the items on the proofreading checklist.

- Unless you are writing a process (how-to-do) essay, eliminate "you" from your writing.

- Make sure every sentence (except for process essays) contains an expressed subject and a verb.

- Skip lines so that you can make corrections later.

- Practice, practice, practice!! The more you write, the better the writer you will become.

NARRATIVE ESSAYS

Narration is the most common form of communication. After seeing a movie, we often summarize the plot for our friends. If something unexpected happens to us (winning a prize, having an accident, witnessing a bank robbery), we most certainly communicate what happened and/or how we felt at the moment of the action. Most of the articles that we read in newspapers and magazines are narrations of events that have taken place around the world. They may be humorous or serious. Regardless, the choice of words used will set the tone. Use a thesaurus to help you select just the right word to convey the tone.

There is no set number of words for an effective piece of narrative writing. It can be a short joke or a long novel. When writers use the third person ("he," "she," or "they") in writing biographies, they may interview the person(s) involved in the action and then convey their findings to their readers. In so doing, the writer must make his/her audience understand what others have experienced. When a reporter views a "story in the making" and cannot interview the people, he has to guess how they feel. These accounts often are based on what the writer observes the participants' reactions to be in a situation.

However, when writers are the persons who experience the action, they may find it easier to communicate their emotions directly to the readers to make them understand them better. These autobiographical accounts are written in the first person ("I," "we").

Often they are difficult to write, particularly if there is a great deal of emotional stress involved in the events being discussed. First-person narrators can get so involved in telling the whole story of their experience that they include too many details and detract from the story that they are trying to relate. Each detail needs to be an integral part of the story and not represent shorter, isolated events. They create dialogues (using direct speech) to express the emotions critical to the action.

Readers want human interest stories, so writers must describe something that will catch their attention and hold it all the way to the end. As you acquire more skills through practice, you will be able to develop an essay that keeps your audience in suspense until the very end.

The first paragraph of your essay is crucial in catching your readers' attention, so take care in making it interesting. In relating the narrative, use chronological order to show logical sequence of each action. Use the appropriate transition words to show this order of events. Your brainstorming beforehand will enable you to organize the events in the order in which they occurred. Changing this order could result in a different outcome for the story. To eliminate any of them might confuse your audience.

Since you will be providing many details in narrating the story, the number of words you use will probably be more than those of previous essays. Regardless, do not worry about the total word count. Just make your readers relive the events with you. Journalists always keep six question words in mind: *who, what, why, when, where,* and *how.* If you answer all of these questions in detail, you will have the basis for a good essay. Do not make each paragraph of your essay an individual story. Be sure that all of the details relate to one central event.

When you have finished your rough draft, ask someone to read it for clarity. Check with your reader to see if your words have conveyed the desired emotions. Did you make your readers feel what you felt as the events were evolving?

As you brainstorm your ideas, relive the event(s) in your own mind. Write down the sequence of events, and beside each indicate the emotion you felt when each one was happening. As you prepare to write, try to find words in your thesaurus that will convey this emotion. Do not write, "I was afraid," but rather say, "The heavy footsteps below my bedroom window made the hair on my neck stand straight up!" (sent cold shivers up my spine; caused me to tremble uncontrollably). These expressions make your readers *feel* as you felt.

Steps to Follow in Writing Narrative Essays

- Use topics of human interest.

- Let your readers know by the tone you use in your introductory paragraph whether your narrative will be serious or humorous.

- Focus on a particular event and what led up to it.

- Focus on the feelings and reactions of those involved.

- Tell how you or they felt at the precise moment.

- In a third-person account, focus on what you see: faces, emotions, reactions, and so on.

- Catch your readers' attention from the very start of the essay.

- Keep your readers' attention by building up and creating more interest in the event.

- Provide many details.

- Make it more realistic by using direct speech and quoting people's exact words.

- Once you have reached the peak of the action, gradually bring your story to a close.

- Don't write an abrupt ending.

- Don't try to be funny when the event is serious or tragic.

- Use a thesaurus to find just the right word to describe the emotional impact.

- Keep events in chronological order.

EXERCISE 49

Read the following narrative "Escape," and see what details the writer provided. Then answer the questions based on the essay.

1. Is the title an attention getter?
yes, it is.

2. When you see the title "Escape" what do you expect to read?
I expected to read about someone running away.

3. What does the first sentence make you anticipate about what follows?
As Angela and their children arrived at the airport that hot August day

4. What details create an emotional response? *the sight of the rifle-toting paramilita*

5. What details in the opening paragraph catch your attention?

6. Find the details that convey the emotions of the story.

7. Do you think that the narrative is too dramatic? Is it real?

8. Does the writer hold your attention to the very end?

9. Why do you think that they were running away?

10. Has something in your life caused you great fear? How did you handle the situation?

Keep the following points in mind as you read the essay:

Purpose:	to share a personal experience with others
Audience:	instructor, single parents, other students
Method:	narrative
Thesis Statement:	Nothing must happen to her and the children if they were to reach their homeland before her husband found them missing.

Escape

As Angela and her children arrived at the airport that hot August day, the sight of the rifle-toting paramilitary police made her very apprehensive. Their presence was another aspect of this foreign culture that had troubled her during her four-year residence. Would they detain her and the children, demand the special letter she should be carrying but was not, search her luggage in an effort to delay her, possibly causing them to miss their flight? Nothing must happen to her and the children if they were to reach their homeland before her husband found them missing. Shortly after presenting their tickets at the check-in desk, she heard an announcement about the delay in their flight. Her brain swam with the horrors that would befall them if they were caught. Imagining herself and her children imprisoned and abandoned, left to die in a dark and damp cell, made her shake and break out in a cold sweat despite the scorching temperatures in the small and crowded airport. Twenty, thirty, forty minutes passed before the announcement of a new departure time—5:20—another agonizing thirty minutes. Her palms began to sweat; her hands shook; the walls seemed to close in on her as she tried to compose herself.

Ten minutes later the passengers pushed their way to the Passport Control. How carefully would the police scrutinize the documents? Would they require the letter of permission needed to get the children out of the country? Why were they taking so long? Why was the policeman looking at her that way, she wondered.

The officer picked up the rubber stamp, but hesitated before using it. He looked at her and then at the children and compared them and the faces on the document. The children were wide-eyed, anxious, and frightened as they fidgeted in front of the official. The few seconds seemed like an eternity before he stamped the two small green passports.

As she and the three children boarded the plane, she felt somewhat relieved. Freedom was only nine hours away, a period that would be far less traumatic than the two hours spent in the airport. No words can describe the joys of freedom.

VOCABULARY EXPANSION

rifle-toting – carrying rifles

detain – to stop

befall – to come someone's way, happen

scorching – very hot

hesitated – paused

traumatic – causing great emotional pain

DISCUSSION EXERCISE

Before you begin to read the essay "Strange Names for Food," look at the title. 1) What do you think the writer will be discussing? 2) What tone will this essay have: serious, humorous, sarcastic? 3) Have you ever experienced some of the same things as the reader? 4) How do you feel about trying new and different foods? 5) What is your favorite American food? 6) When did you first try it? 7) What American foods have you tried and not liked?

Before you read this essay, keep the following points in mind:

Purpose:	entertain with a personal experience
Audience:	other foreign students, tourists, instructor
Method:	narrative
Thesis Statement:	Americans have strange names for their food, and we foreigners never know what to order from a menu.

Strange Names for Food

Americans have strange names for their food, and we foreigners never know what to order from a menu. Last week some of my friends and I went to a restaurant and could not understand the menu. There were no translations and no ingredients listed for some of the dishes. We had been ordering chicken, hamburgers, and fries because we knew what they were, but this restaurant did not have any of those things on the menu.

We realized that Americans had many wonderful foods, so we decided to be daring and order different things without knowing what they were. For our main dish we ordered pigs in a blanket, city chicken, hot dogs, and sloppy joes. We never knew that there was a difference between city and country chickens, but we wanted to find out. To our surprise city chicken is not chicken at all; it's veal served on a stick! Pigs in a blanket are little sausages wrapped in pastry dough and cooked in the oven. Hot dogs are not dog meat, but rather something made with beef and pork. The sloppy joes were a slightly messy sandwich with a mixture of ground meat and tomato sauce on a sandwich bun. At home we don't usually eat our food with our fingers, but all three of these dishes were to be eaten with our hands.

Our next order was for dessert. Some restaurants have those nice plastic picture menus so you can see what you are getting, but not this one. We decided to try something different. The menu offered devil's food cake, angel food cake, grasshopper pie, sponge cake, and pineapple upside-down cake. Now, who would want to have grasshoppers and sponges for dessert, and who would turn a cake upside down with all the good frosting on the bottom? Then we debated on who would be the devils and who would be the angels and why they would call these desserts by those names. Each of us decided to order something different, and what a surprise we got when we saw the choices!

We decided to order iced tea because the mixed drinks included a screwdriver, a warrior's itch, a pink squirrel, a rusty nail, a bloody Mary, and a brandy Alexander. We weren't brave enough to try any of these!

Our adventure that afternoon was definitely a lesson in culture shock, and we laughed all the way home. One of my friends is making a list of these strange names and will probably buy a cookbook to find out what the ingredients are.

VOCABULARY EXPANSION

devil's food cake – chocolate cake

angel food cake – a spongy white cake made with egg whites

sponge cake – like angel food cake but with more flavoring

grasshopper pie – a creamy pie with peppermint flavoring and green color

pineapple upside-down cake – made with pineapple rings lining the bottom of the pan with a glazed cherry inside each ring. When the cake has cooled, the cook turns it upside down on a platter so that when it is served, the pineapple rings and cherries are on top.

Keep the following points in mind as you read the essay "An Act of Love."

Purpose:	to show that all Americans are not rich; to indicate how people got together to help someone in trouble
Audience:	other students and instructor
Method:	narrative
Thesis statement:	In times of trouble, people are helping others to cope and to survive.

Look at the outline that a student wrote for this essay.

I. Oklahoma farmer is about to lose his farm.

    A. Bank forecloses.

    B. Marshal and deputies arrive.

    C. Friends blockade the property.

    D. Deputies retreat.

II. Newspaper reports events.

    A. People are outraged.

    B. Bank manager is cruel.

    C. People send money.

    D. Check for $5000 arrives.

    E. Man regains farm.

CONCLUSION: This incident restores man's faith in man to come to his rescue in times of trouble.

An Act of Love (I)

Many people think of the United States as a land of plenty. They think that poverty and starvation do not exist. Others find these to be everyday occurrences. Suddenly, many people are losing their homes and their land. In times of trouble, people are helping others to cope and to survive.

Recently, a 65-year-old Oklahoma farmer was about to lose his farm. The bank was foreclosing on his mortgage. The farmer could not pay, so the bank, which owned the land, wanted to take it away. He was very much upset because his family had owned and farmed the land for more than sixty years. It was the only home he had ever known.

The manager of the bank refused to listen to reason. He sent a marshal and his deputies to the property to evict the man and his family. Many of the farmer's friends armed themselves with shotguns. They declared their loyalty to their friends and blockaded the advance of the officials. Finally, the marshal and his deputies retreated.

Newspapers across the country reported this event. Many people were outraged that a man who had farmed that land for so many years should have to leave it. They thought that the bank manager had been very cruel to the man, who was too old to work at anything else. People from east to west began sending money—a few dollars here and there, and more from those who could afford it. Suddenly, the farmer needed only $2,500 to pay off the whole mortgage. An anonymous donor sent a check for $5,000. This money allowed the farmer to repay his debt and buy some much-needed equipment.

The bank could no longer bother the farmer because he now owned the land. He had not lost his life's work, and he could still provide food for the people across the country. This incident restored man's faith in man to come to his rescue in times of trouble.

DISCUSSION EXERCISE

Answer these questions as they relate to the story and your personal life: 1) How did you respond emotionally to this story? 2) Can you relate a similar incident that happened in your country? 3) What do people in your country do to help one another out during periods of difficulty? 4) What did you think about when you saw the title of this essay? 5) Did the content surprise you?

VOCABULARY EXPANSION

foreclose – to demand to repay a debt

mortgage – claim on property given to bank that lent the money to buy it

marshal – special police officer

evict – to remove by force

retreated – left

outraged – greatly offended

blockaded – closed off an area; refused to allow entrance

anonymous – unknown or nameless

The following version of "An Act of Love" was written with a great deal of dialogue. Look at how the story comes alive and allows readers to feel more of the emotion that the characters themselves experienced.

An Act of Love (II)

For many American farmers, the thought of losing their farms and their life's work is devastating. Only a few years ago, Mr. Jake Sanders, a 65-year-old Oklahoma farmer, faced the same dilemma. One day, he turned white and shook uncontrollably as he answered the telephone and heard the bank manager say, "Mr. Sanders, I am very sorry to have to do this. Since you have not paid your mortgage in the last two months, our bank is forced to foreclose. You have thirty days to vacate the premises."

Mrs. Sanders was worried when she saw the look on her husband's face. "What's the matter?" she asked as she watched him fall limply into the overstuffed chair.

"The bank is taking away our house and everything we have worked hard to own in the last forty-five years. We have no place to go."

She sobbed at the thought of leaving the homestead that they loved and had worked so hard to preserve. Mr. Sanders's father had worked the land for twenty years, and now his son had worked another forty-five years, only to lose it to the bank.

News traveled fast in the small town, and the Sanderses' friends came to visit. Suddenly, a marshal and his deputies appeared on the property. The marshal said, "I have orders to serve this eviction notice. You must leave in thirty days."

Upset by this news, Mr. Sanders's friends picked up their shotguns and said, "Go away and don't come back. This is their land, and we're here to see that it continues to be theirs. They have no other jobs and are too old to do anything else. Get out of here!"

After firing a few shots in the air, they managed to scare off the deputies.

A reporter happened to be in the area and filmed the scene. He said on his broadcast, "This is a shame to treat an old man so badly. The bank manager is so greedy that he thrives on making the poor suffer. We need to do something about this."

Suddenly, the station telephones started ringing and people from many parts of the country were calling and donating money to help the farmer make the payments on his land. An anonymous donor said, "I'm sending $5,000 to help Mr. Sanders save his land. I hope he never has to deal with the bank again."

The farmer paid off his mortgage and had enough left over to buy some much-needed equipment. The bank could do nothing because he now owned the land, and no one could take it away from him. This incident restored man's faith in man to come to his rescue in times of trouble.

VOCABULARY EXPANSION

dilemma – very difficult situation that forces one to make a choice

vacate – to leave a place permanently

premises – land and building on it; property

limply – unsteadily

sobbed – cried uncontrollably

homestead – usually a farmhouse and land

thieves – people who steal from others

WRITING EXERCISE

Find a newspaper or magazine article that narrates a human interest story. Underline the answers the story contains to the journalistic questions who, what, why, when, where, and how. Look at the introductory statements and how the writer gets his readers' attention. Explain why the article attracted your attention.

WRITING EXERCISE

In an encyclopedia or an online source, read a short biographical sketch of a famous person and see what interesting information the writer presents. Tell why you selected this particular biography.

> ## WRITING EXERCISE
>
> In a magazine, read a first-person human interest story. Notice the writing techniques that the author used. Mention some of them. Did the dialogue make you feel more a part of the action? Did the narrator create suspense? What did the writer do to hold your attention?

> ## WRITING EXERCISE
>
> Select two of the following topics and write a narrative essay on each.

- A wonderful surprise

- An unforgettable vacation (the event)

- The frustration of registering for classes

- A frightening experience

- Your first experience in an American restaurant

- An interesting (inspiring, admirable) person whom you have met personally (narrate the event)

- An embarrassing (unforgettable) moment

- A funny experience resulting from your limited knowledge of English

DESCRIPTION ESSAYS

For many, description essays are the most exciting to read because, if well written, they provide numerous details that make the writing come alive. However, they are also the most difficult for beginners to write. The key to composing a good description essay is to spend a great deal of time brainstorming and using a thesaurus to find the exact word that best describes the image that the writers are trying to convey to their readers. To say that something is specifically red, yellow, or blue only eliminates the other colors of the rainbow. A thesaurus contains at least 80 entries to represent different shades of each color. Indigo, navy, and turquoise are all blue hues, but they represent different intensities of the color. Love has many forms, and there are many ways to describe the intensity of this emotion. Choosing the right word will convey the appropriate meaning you are looking for and will save you some possible embarrassment from not checking out the vocabulary more closely.

There also exists a difference between a factual and a personal description. The former is more formal and analyzes the subject from corner to corner as if you were describing a photograph. The passive voice is often used in such descriptions.

Personal description, on the other hand, is more concerned with action and emotion. Writers, as well as readers, are concerned with who is doing something and how he/she feels when he is doing it. Through a series of well-chosen transition words, writers can move smoothly from place to place or from time to time. Emphasis is on the senses, what the characters hear, see, smell, feel, and taste. Well-chosen words make the audience share the emotions of the central figures in the unfolding drama.

Although you know yourself better than anyone else does, it can be very difficult to write about yourself and your experiences. Both your purpose in writing the essay and the audience to whom you are appealing play a major role in the choice of words you use, your tone, and presentation. If you were writing a grant proposal to fund a project of great interest to you, you would accentuate your achievements, goals, and the ways you would use the newly acquired knowledge to help others. However, if a friend offers to get you a date for the most important social event of the year, you will emphasize your physical attributes and your likes and dislikes.

During the brainstorming process, write as many adjectives as you can to describe an object, a situation, or a person. Focus on only one aspect of your topic so that you can do a good job in a short period of time. It is better to have too many adjectives than too few. Build from small to large, from least to most important, and from common to exciting. Try to make your readers sit on the edge of their seats, waiting for your next fascinating detail to appear. Make them see what you see. Keep the following steps in mind as you write.

Steps to Follow in Writing a Description Essay

- Focus on the topic.

- Be very familiar with the topic.

- Set a picture in front of you as you write so that you will be able to provide all the necessary details.

- Brainstorm. Write as many details as come to mind.

- Narrow the scope of your description. If describing a person or a city, focus on one or two aspects.

- Eliminate all description not directly related to your topic.

- Check a thesaurus for words that mean the same as the ones you want to use. This will eliminate the monotonous repetition of vocabulary.

- Start from the least important detail and build to the most important to create more interest.

- Write a concluding paragraph that sums up the description.

- If possible, attach a picture so that your reader can appreciate the imagery as much as you have.

- Remember that descriptions focus on people or things, not on events.

DISCUSSION EXERCISE

Read the first essay, which describes the physical characteristics of the men from Taquile Island, to see how many adjectives the writer used to make the description more vivid. If you closed your eyes and someone read this description to you, would you "see" the same picture? What makes the men in the picture different from the people you are used to seeing in the American city where you now live? Are they different from the men in your hometown? What sort of picture would your readers get if you left out about twenty-five adjectives from the description?

Vest

Chullo

Los Taquileños

> Read the beginning of the next essay, which describes the men's attire, and fill in the necessary information to make it complete. To help yourself in this task, look at the accompanying picture and brainstorm every article of clothing that you see them wearing, before you begin to describe them. Think of as many adjectives and details as you can so that your description comes alive.
>
> Next, locate on a map Lake Titicaca, Peru, and Bolivia. Read some information on these areas, the history, and the present inhabitants. Then consult a thesaurus on materials and textures to help you choose the words to describe the men's clothing. Use the vocabulary below to help you make your word choices.

Considering that *los taquileños* live on a small island at 12,500 feet (some 3,750 meters) above sea level, what sorts of materials and textures would be found in their clothing? How would you describe the following types of materials? Which ones would they be most likely to use?

alpaca, cotton, flannel, fleece, gauze, homespun, lace, linen, llama, mohair, silk, sackcloth, satin, suede, velour, vicuna, wool.

Some other vocabulary to consider:

grain: fine, coarse, soft, shiny, furry, nappy, spun, heavy, light, loosely/tightly woven

length: elbow, sleeves, yoke, waist, ankle, V-neck

The material for the garments is coarse and made from llama wool. It is homespun on a small loom. The hat is a *chullo*, knitted by the men of the island.

Purpose:	to describe interesting and different people from Peru
Audience:	instructor, other students, people interested in other cultures, tourists
Method:	description
Thesis Statement:	They were interesting men in both their physical appearance and way of life. They were different, and that was what attracted me to them.

These two essays describe *los taquileños*, the men from Taquile Island, Peru, from two different points of view. The first, provided in its entirety, analyzes their physical appearance, the second their clothing. Read the first to see how many adjectives the writer used to make the description more vivid. For the second, look at the accompanying pictures and, using the new vocabulary, finish writing the essay.

Los Taquileños

Los taquileños were men whom I met on Lake Titicaca in Peru four years ago. Their facial features were pure Indian. Like the natives of this region, they had high cheekbones, almond-shaped eyes, and aquiline noses. The harsh weather had taken its toll on their dark, craggy skin. Perhaps they were descendants of the great Incas, whom Pizarro had conquered in 1534. What would have been their fate had their ancestors continued to live the happy and carefree life that they had enjoyed in the twelfth century? Los taquileños were the pilot crew of the motorboat that took us across Lake Titicaca on that cold winter day. They were proud men, as one could see in their noble bearing—proud of their heritage, proud of their lifestyle, proud and conscientious of their job. Their hands were strong as they maneuvered the wheel of the launch. Nothing seemed to distract them as they concentrated on taking us safely across the large lake. The song they sang was in Quechua, their native language. They spoke little Spanish, which made our conversation very limited. As they smiled, they displayed even white teeth, an unusual characteristic for this part of the world. Despite their short stature, probably no more than five feet four inches, they stood tall and regal. Los taquileños were the epitome of the true modern-day Inca, but to me they were different and interesting.

VOCABULARY EXPANSION

los taquileños – men from Taquile Island, Peru

Lake Titicaca – body of water 12,500 feet above sea level located between Peru and Bolivia

features – physical aspects of the face

aquiline – curving like the beak of an eagle

harsh – rough; severe

craggy – rugged; rough

take its toll – create undesirable effects

heritage – traditions passed on by one's ancestors

conscientious – careful; diligent; devoted to doing a good job

maneuvered – steered

launch – small, open motorboat

Quechua – ancient Indian language spoken in Peru

stature – height

regal – splendid; magnificent; royal

epitome – typical example of something

fate – destiny

descendant – your child, grandchild, or great-grandchild, and so on

homespun – simple, made at home

loom – a device for weaving cloth

A Different Costume

These noble gentlemen are wearing garments typical of those worn by the inhabitants of Taquile Island in Peru. They knitted the *chullo* (cap) that they are wearing. It is multicolored, with earflaps and with a tassel at the end. These clothes protect them against the intense cold of this high Andean region. The geometric design is one of many that these people incorporate into their caps, vests, and belts.

They also made their homespun shirts and pants. _____

_____

_____

_____

_____

_____

_____

Their way of dressing seems unusual to us, but it is very practical for the cold and windy region where these men live and work.

WRITING EXERCISES

- Write some descriptions that appeal to the emotions. Get some ideas from articles that you find in magazines or newspapers.

- Find a photograph from your album or a picture in a magazine and describe what is happening. It will be easier to write about something involving action than one representing still life.

- Look at another photo or magazine picture and create a story. Answer the six journalistic questions who, what, why, when, where, and how.

- Select two of the following topics and write an essay on each.

  The most beautiful city I have ever visited

  The joy of summer, fall, winter (spring was developed earlier)

  My dream house

  The ideal man or woman

  A letter to a friend in your country describing life in the United States

  The thrill of the first snowfall

  A train ride through the mountains

  Being in love

POINT OF VIEW

The point of view from which you create your story is very important in presenting just the right description. As you grow older, your perspective changes, and so do the words you use to describe what you see and feel. Think about some of the things from your childhood: toys, friends, acquaintances, places, or your house. Write a brief description of two of these things from your point of view as a child. Look at this writer's account of the house she lived in until she was ten years old. As you read, circle the words or phrases that appeal to the senses.

My Childhood Home

I remember the large old three-story house of my early youth. It seemed so big. We had a very spacious, open basement with a coal bin under the steps. An old man with gray hair and a gray beard used to shovel coal through an outside opening into the bin once a month. It was cold in our basement, and I hated to go down there. My mother had an old-fashioned wringer washing machine down there. She would spend hours just washing and hanging clothes. She always seemed so tired on those days.

When we sat in the roomy kitchen, everything seemed so high and out of reach. There was a small light fixture on the wall above the table and another smaller one over the sink. The dining room was beautiful, with its long white lacy curtains, which my mother would soak in a starch solution and then dry on special racks in the sun. My brother, sister, and I could never stay in that room because it was just for grownups. ~~adults~~ When our parents entertained, we would sit at the top of the steps and peek through the wooden railing to see what was going on. Sometimes we would stay there so long that we would fall asleep, and our father would carry us to bed. This was the first house I remember. It was filled with laughter and joy despite our lack of material things.

Now look at the same writing from the author's point of view many years later as she revisited the house as an adult.

A Return Visit to My Childhood Home

As I returned to our old house many years later, I still recalled the laughter and good times of my youth. However, I looked at the changes the owners had made over the years. The children were gone, and an older couple lived there alone. The old basement was warm and cheery, with a small sitting room and a television to replace the old coal bin. We never had a television because it was too expensive. A new gold-colored washer and dryer replaced my mother's old hand-driven machine. Modern technology has made life easier for this family. The lovely yellow-dotted ruffled curtains brighten the whole area.

As I go from room to room and remember our lives there, I look more at the changes that have taken place. The kitchen does not seem so large. Is it that I have grown so much taller? Could it be that modern technology allows for drop ceilings and fluorescent lighting to create an illusion? I am an adult now, but I will not attend any of the parties held in the dining room. The old toy chest by the big bay window has been replaced by several winding plant stands containing fragrant gardenias, yellow daisies, and coral roses.

I cry as I leave the old house I haven't seen in thirty-five years. The memories are there, but the house has changed. I, too, have changed with time.

DISCUSSION EXERCISE

1) What were some of the feelings that the writer created in the first account? 2) Had she been a child living in the house thirty-five years later, would she have felt the brightness, warmth, and cheeriness of the basement? 3) Would modern technology have created as much of an impression on the writer as the absence of it did? 4) Would her mother's modern laundry chores have created as lasting an impression as her use of the old hand-driven machine did? 5) What change might have affected her the most?

One student chose "Wonders of Winter" as a topic for one of her essays. The following shows her pre-writing activities.

BRAINSTORMING FOR WONDERS OF WINTER

snow

sports—participation

skiing, tobogganing, skating, sledding, building snowmen, building igloos

crisp air

beauty of snowflakes, icicles

sleigh rides

special clothing

holidays—Thanksgiving, Christmas, Kwanzaa, Hanukkah, New Year's Day

football games

twinkling star-filled sky

ice formations

cold

long walks

children at play

travel difficulties

snowball fights

accidents, hazards

fireplace—cozy, romantic

tinkling of seasonal bells

romanticism

Regrouping and eliminating

sports and activities	physical aspects	romantic
participation-spectator	snow	long walks
skiing	icicles	sleigh rides
tobogganing	ice forms	fireplace
skating	hazards	holidays
football season	crisp air	twinkling stars
holiday game		tinkling bells
televised Olympics		
snowball fights		
building snowmen and igloos		
sledding		

As you begin a writing assignment, reserve enough time for brainstorming. Coming up with the information for all of the details you want to include in your essay will require much thought. You will then have to regroup your ideas and possibly eliminate some, being careful to include only those that develop the main idea of each paragraph.

Wonders of Winter (Adults)

Thesis Statement: Hopeless romantics find the nostalgia of winter to be calming and inspirational.

I. Feeling of tranquillity

    A. Long walks

    B. Sleigh rides

    C. Tinkling bells and twinkling lights

II. Inspirational period

    A. Holidays

        1. Thanksgiving

        2. Hanukkah, Christmas, and Kwanzaa

        3. New Year's Day

    B. Fire in the fireplace

    C. Star gazing

Conclusion: Among its many wonders, winter provides a feeling of tranquillity and a time for inspiration.

Wonders of Winter (Children)

Thesis Statement: Winter is the most wonderful time of the year for children.

I. Unique activities

    A. Making snowmen

    B. Having snowball fights

    C. Building igloos

    D. Sledding

II. Children's smiles

    A. Holidays

    B. Visit with Santa Claus

    C. Decorations

    D. Vacation

Conclusion: The other seasons of the year offer exciting things for children, but none is as wonderful as the activities of winter. Winter is for them the greatest time of the year.

Purpose:	To describe the thrill that adults feel with the simple pleasures of winter and to show that despite the cold and hazardous conditions that can exist, winter can be a peaceful and inspirational period to ponder the wonders of nature and to provide people with a time for self-evaluation.
Audience:	primarily those adults who reject the wonders of the season; your instructor; those who have never experienced a snowy North American winter.
Method:	description
Thesis Statement:	Hopeless romantics find the nostalgia of winter to be calming and inspirational.

Wonders of Winter (adult)

In many parts of the world there are four distinct seasons. For many, winter is the most wonderful of all. Hopeless romantics find the nostalgia of winter to be calming and inspirational. Outdoor enthusiasts enjoy the seasonal activities. The sights and sounds of the season provide a special attraction for all.

Activities on a snowy winter night provide a feeling of tranquillity. Many people take long walks through a quiet area to find peace. Soon they forget the turmoil of the job or classroom and enjoy the carefree atmosphere. Sleigh rides bring out the best in the romantics. Cozy and warm under a blanket shared with a special friend, they pass through the open countryside and savor the beauty of the area. The tinkling of bells and the twinkling lights in the distance create a euphoria that will carry them through difficult moments during the week that follows.

Winter is also an inspirational period. It is the season for Thanksgiving, Hanukkah, Kwanzaa, and Christmas. Thanksgiving comes in late November, when most cold regions have already experienced their first heavy snowfall. The holiday is a time to count blessings and give thanks for the events of the past year. For many, it is a time to reflect on where they have been and where they are going. Hanukkah, Christmas, and Kwanzaa are all celebrated in December. Christians and Jews enjoy religious holidays and then recall the hardships of the original celebrants of these feasts. It is also a joyous time of giving. Quiet moments encourage meditation. Outdoors, twinkling stars in a dark blue sky on a crisp winter night focus the attention of stargazers on the heavens and the wonders of the universe: walking on the moon, outer-space travel, and other life forms. Winter is truly the most wonderful season for peace, meditation, and joy.

VOCABULARY EXPANSION

distinct – different, unique

nostalgia – desire to return to a place of the past associated with fond memories

tranquillity – peace

turmoil – commotion

sleigh – horse-drawn carriage on runners

tinkling – jingling, metallic sound—like little bells ringing

twinkling – sparkling, lit up

Kwanzaa – an African-American cultural festival in December

stargazers – people who watch the movement of the stars

Hanukkah – a Jewish festival of lights that usually takes place in December

euphoria – feeling of happiness and well-being

Purpose:	to describe how many North American children celebrate winter.
Audience:	children who have never experienced a snowy North American winter; your instructor.
Method:	description
Thesis Statement:	Winter is the most wonderful time of the year for children.

Wonders of Winter (child)

Each season has a special meaning for many people. Winter is the most wonderful time of the year for children. There are many outdoor activities that thrill children of all ages. A variety of holidays that offer them the freedom to do what they want provide a great deal of excitement for them.

Children living in cold regions can participate in activities unique to this season. The joy on children's faces as the first snow falls is like no other. There is a great deal of chatter and excitement in the air. Seeing several inches of snow on the ground sends them rushing out to build a snowman and to have snowball fights with their friends. They build igloos and pretend to be Eskimos living in the far regions of North America. Their fathers and older brothers drag out the sleds and pull the children for long distances. They even slide down icy hills in the parks.

What could be more delightful than to see the smiles of children throughout December as they prepare to celebrate Hanukkah, Christmas, and Kwanzaa! As they await the big day, their thoughts turn to the gifts they hope to receive. For some, a visit to see Santa Claus is a big event. They experience a great thrill as they read about the jolly old man and his sleigh pulled by eight reindeer. The sound of Christmas carols fills the air. Red, green, and white lights twinkle all over town as the decorations announce the approaching holiday season. One of the biggest joys of winter for children is to have a two-week vacation from school to play all day.

The other seasons of the year offer exciting things for children, but none are as wonderful as the activities of winter. Most youngsters can spend their vacation time outdoors, enjoying the cold-weather sports. The colored lights and sounds created by the holidays increase their enjoyment. Winter is the greatest time of all for children.

VOCABULARY EXPANSION

chatter – excited talking, especially among children

rushing – hurrying

igloo – ice house for Eskimos

carols – Christmas songs

Hanukkah – a Jewish festival of lights that usually takes place in December

Kwanza – an African-American cultural festival which takes place in December

jolly – happy

thrill – excitement

> ## WRITING EXERCISE
>
> Select one of the following topics and write two essays, one from the perspective of a child, and the other from that of an adult.

- First day of school in kindergarten and high school

- Returning to your high school for the class reunion (atmosphere as student and as graduate)

- Valentine's Day as a child and as an adult

- Your first job and your first job as a professional

- Returning to a town you have not visited in a number of years

- Seeing an old and dear friend after many years (friend before and after)

- Analyzing a situation from two points of view

- A trip to Disney World from child's and adult's perspective

PROCESS ESSAYS

A process essay gives step-by-step directions for doing something, like learning to surf or how to play the guitar. Reading one is like following a recipe.

Although process analysis is probably easier to write, it takes much more forethought and planning than other essay types. You must think out all the details and list them in the proper order before you write the thesis statement. Never try to tell anyone how to do something unless you are somewhat of an expert at doing it yourself. If you come to a certain point of the paper and say, "I think this comes next, or maybe it comes later," you have lost your readers' attention. Anyone planning to make something wants to do it in the shortest period of time and in the least complicated manner, with the assurance that his efforts will be successful. Trying to backtrack by saying, "Oh, I forgot to mention that you have to do this first," only frustrates your readers in their attempts to follow the instructions.

In composing this essay, you should pretend that you are giving a live demonstration. As you write, keep in mind the audience you are addressing. After all, you would not want to present Einstein's Theory of Relativity to a group of third graders.

If there is a need to explain why you are doing something or using a particular tool in a given step, explain it. You want everything to be perfectly clear so that your readers will also be successful in creating something new.

Your thesis statement should tell your readers what you are planning to do, how you are going to do it, and what items they will need to accomplish the task. Make your introduction interesting so that the readers will want to continue. If they see that the items needed are difficult to find or that they are too expensive, they will not continue to read the essay. Use one or two key words (adjectives or adverbs) that will be the theme of the paper.

The following introductory paragraphs give several key words that catch the readers' attention and make them want to read the whole essay in order to learn the process involved.

Changing a tire on a deserted country road can be a frightening experience, but by following these simple steps and having on hand a good spare tire, a jack, and a flashlight or lantern, you can complete the task easily and quickly.

Easily and *quickly* are the words that catch the readers' attention, and the three required articles are those which all drivers should have in the trunks of their cars. Readers will most likely learn in the essay how to change a tire easily and quickly.

Steps to Follow in Writing Process Essays

- Think about your topic. Are you somewhat of an expert in this area? If not, choose another one.

- Is this a topic that will interest your readers?

- Remember your audience.

- Brainstorm and list all the steps necessary to complete the task.

- Rearrange all the steps in chronological order.

- Run through the process in your own mind to make sure that you have not missed anything.

- Eliminate any unnecessary procedures.

- Think of an interesting beginning paragraph and a thesis statement that will attract your readers' attention. You can always change this later, but at least it will keep you focused on the process.

- Write your thesis statement telling what you will do, how you will do it, and what equipment you will need.

- Review the transition words that will make your ideas flow from one paragraph to the next: *you begin by, first, second, then, after this, next, finally,* and *the last step.*

- Explain how to use all the necessary tools, any technical vocabulary, and the visible results, if any, at each step of the way.

- Pretend that you are following this process by reading what you have written.

- Does the process flow smoothly? Did you eliminate anything?

- Write a conclusion that sums up the process and lets your readers know that you have finished the project.

- Do not end abruptly.

- Reread the whole paper, concentrating on spelling, grammar, and topic development.

Grammar Review

Since the process paper is intended to tell someone how to do something, most of what you write will be in the command form. All command forms (familiar, formal, singular, plural) are the same with *you* as the subject understood. To make the affirmative command for all verbs, take the infinitive and drop the *to*.

~~TO~~ BE   ~~TO~~ GO   ~~TO~~ ADD   ~~TO~~ MIX   ~~TO~~ NAIL

For negative commands add *don't* to the above mentioned forms.

DON'T BE   **DON'T GO**   **DON'T ADD**   **DON'T MIX**   **DON'T NAIL**

Other commands not usually used in this type of writing are the group commands, which include the speaker as part of the group.

LET'S MIX   **LET'S PLANT**   **LET'S BUY**

The negative form simply places *not* between *let's* and the verb.

LET'S NOT MIX   **LET'S NOT PLANT**   **LET'S NOT BUY**

Read the following introductory paragraphs and underline the key words that catch the reader's attention. Also locate the tools or materials needed to complete the process.

Sample Thesis Statements for a Process Essay

How to excel in school

Achieving success in later life is the goal of many people today. This accomplishment has its roots in high school and college. *Being a successful student is not something that comes overnight, but one that requires patience, hard work, accepting responsibility, and determination. Following these steps can help a person excel in school.*

How to meet a man or woman

Do you find life a bit lonely and dull? Are all of your friends having fun while you sit home on weekends? Don't be discouraged. *Just follow these easy steps and you, too, will be able to meet interesting people. All you need are a pencil and paper to jot down some desirable characteristics about the person you want to meet, an inventory of your wardrobe, a full-length mirror, and a personal evaluation.*

How to buy a used car

Because the price of new cars is drastically increasing every year, many people have taken to buying used cars. Many of them get only a piece of junk, while others obtain real bargains. *If you want to be among the latter, follow these easy steps. The only things your initial search will require are a newspaper, a notebook and a pencil, a blue book (a book listing the current values of used cars), and a knowledge of basic mechanics.*

How to conserve energy in a house

With the soaring costs of heating and cooling, and the ever-increasing scarcity of natural gas, Americans are seeking ways to conserve energy. *This process can become less frustrating and more economical by following these steps. All you will need are an inventory of home appliances, a survey of windows and doors, a long, hard look at last year's bills, and a family conference on ways to conserve energy.*

The essay below, "Saving Money at the Supermarket," is a timely topic, since all of us are trying to economize on our food purchases.

1) Is this essay helpful to you in your attempts to save money?

2) How many steps are involved in this process?

3) What transition words does the writer use this time?

4) Do you think that the writer's advice is good?

Purpose:	to emphasize the need to be budget conscious and how to find ways to economize on grocery shopping
Audience:	instructor, other students, members of the community
Method:	process
Thesis Statement:	To get the most for their dollar, all they need to start their shopping venture are a pen, a piece of paper, the grocery ads from the local newspaper, a pair of scissors, and a hand calculator.

Saving Money at the Supermarket

Many Americans are budget conscious and try to save money on everything that they purchase. They find that they can do without new clothes, luxury items, new cars, and a variety of other items. However, food is an integral part of their lifestyle, and few are willing to sacrifice completely at the grocery store. In an effort to cut back on grocery spending, they must devise a plan that includes writing lists, comparing products, and searching for bargains. To get the most for their dollar, all they need to start their shopping venture are a pen, a piece of paper, the grocery ads from the local newspaper, a pair of scissors, and a hand calculator.

Once a week the local newspaper runs the weekly grocery ads and provides special discount coupons on a variety of products. This section of the paper is a good source for bargain hunting. Look up the ads for the stores closest to you or the ones you may pass on the way to school or work. Driving across town will consume more gasoline and eat up the savings you might have had elsewhere. Decide on your menus for the week and shop accordingly. You may wish to see what is on sale before you decide on the menus, however. Clip the coupons for the products that you always use, and buy only what you need for the next week, unless it is a super sale and you wish to stock up on items that you use frequently (certain canned goods, toilet tissue, soap, etc.) Once you decide on the menu, calculate how much of each item you will need for the week, and prepare your list. Try to organize your list so that all the items you normally find in one aisle are together. This will save you from running back and forth in the store as you load your grocery cart. Plan to purchase only what is on your list unless the cartful of marked-downed merchandise contains bargain prices on products that you always use. Use your hand calculator to figure price per ounce in deciding whether the sale item is a better buy than the house brand. Don't buy name brands all the time because the company has to pay for the advertising and passes this extra charge along to you, the customer. Never go shopping on an empty stomach. When you are hungry, you tend to buy more than you really need.

Now that you have finished the preliminaries, go to the supermarket and begin your shopping. Start down the first aisle and pick up everything that you need from there, and then proceed to the next aisle. Do not be distracted by other things that you see. Buy only what is on your list.

When you have placed all of the groceries in your cart, head for the checkout. Hand the cashier all of the coupons first, and then watch carefully as the cashier rings up your order. Sometimes the store will give double refunds on individual coupons valued up to one dollar. This could bring additional savings to you. Even though many stores now have scanners, the machines sometimes make mistakes in the store's favor, so be sure that the cashier rings the correct price. After you have put the bags in the car, head for home and double-check the prices against the receipt.

If you follow a set plan, cut out your coupons, prepare your list, and buy only the items you had planned, your shopping trip will be a success, and you will have saved money on your groceries. You will be happy with these savings and will be able to apply the money toward the purchase of something that you need in the future. Everyone can save money at the supermarket and feel the rewards of budget-conscious shopping. Reap your rewards tomorrow!

VOCABULARY EXPANSION

integral – whole

devise – to create

venture – an undertaking

consume – to waste, use up

elsewhere – in another part

sacrifice – to give up something for the good of someone or for a cause

clip – to cut out

preliminaries – things that need to be done or take place first

scanners – machines that copy the product codes and register the prices

reap – to harvest, to see a positive outcome

Read the essay "Summer Gardens," below, and underline the transition words throughout.

1) How many steps are there in this process? Number each one.

2) The thesis statement says that the process will be *easy, money saving,* and *rewarding*. Is it? Indicate the details that support this thesis.

Purpose:	to encourage people to plant their own gardens so that they can economize and eat healthy food
Audience:	instructor, other students, members of the community, health-conscious people
Method:	process
Thesis Statement:	This project can be easy, money saving, and rewarding, and the gardens will provide them with proper nutrition at an affordable price.

Summer Gardens

As the price of produce increases almost daily and people cannot afford store products, many people are now planting their own summer vegetable gardens. They are finding that this project can be easy, money saving, and rewarding, and the gardens will provide them with proper nutrition at an affordable price. Initially, it takes some time and energy, but later it requires only a little daily attention. You, too, can enjoy the benefits of home gardening. To begin your project, you need a nice plot of ground that gets a lot of sun and contains good soil, a number of inexpensive gardening tools, some packets of seeds, and a good supply of water.

When you plant your own garden, you will be more concerned with caring for it and giving it a lot of attention than if you allow someone else to do the job for you. First, clear away any obstructions in the soil, such as rocks, twigs, roots, and weeds. All of this will interfere with the proper growth of your plants. You can do most of this by hand or by using a rake. Now take your shovel if the ground is hard, and dig deeply and loosen the soil in the whole plot. If the texture is sandy, then use a hoe (a gardening tool with a thin, flat blade and a long handle). Loosening the soil makes planting the seeds easier, and it helps the plants absorb the water and other minerals, allowing the roots to spread out more easily.

After you have finished this step, you are ready to plant your seeds. Make sure that you read the package directions carefully. Use a trowel (a small scooping hand tool) to dig deeply into the soil and plant the seeds. Some seeds need less depth but require more room to spread out. Be aware of the planting season. If you plant out of season, your garden will not grow until the following year, if at all. Now that the seeds are in the ground, give them just the right amount of water. Watering too little will dry up your plants as well as stunt their growth. Providing too much moisture will rot the roots and damage the crop. If it does not rain a great deal, then connect the garden hose and water about five minutes every day. Very soon you will see bits of green shoots sprouting above the surface of the soil. Every day your plants will grow a little more until you recognize what you have planted. The package in which your seeds came will give you an idea of how long you must wait to harvest your vegetables. You will know by looking at them whether they are ready to harvest.

Sometimes plants need a little fertilizer to help them grow if the soil does not contain all the nutrients they need. You may also find it necessary to use some insecticides to eliminate some of the insect pests that try to eat your crop before you do.

As you watch your vegetables mature, pick them and wash them very carefully to get rid of any loose soil that may cling to them or any chemical sprays that might adhere to their surface. You are now ready to enjoy the tasty vegetables and calculate the money you have saved. Bon appétit!

VOCABULARY EXPANSION

obstructions – anything blocking or getting in the way

twigs – small branches

weeds – undesirable plant

interfere – hinder, get in the way

plot – small piece of land

stunt – keep from growing

rot – to deteriorate

sprouting – beginning to grow

nutrients – food, nourishment

insecticides – chemical sprays that kill insects

adhere – to stick to

Bon appétit! – a French expression indicating "Enjoy your meal!"

rave – to exclaim with great emotion

shovel – a metal gardening implement with a long handle used to break up the soil

trowel – a small, handheld gardening tool used to move the soil around plants

shoots – small part of the plant that is first to break through the ground

WRITING EXERCISE

Now that you have read these well-thought-out examples of process papers, select one of the topics listed below and write your own essay telling someone how to do something. This may seem very long to you, but remember that you are providing many details and that this is a step-by-step process. Be sure to refer to the checklist provided and explain in detail why you are doing something or why you are using a particular tool.

- Becoming physically fit

- Saving money when shopping in a grocery store

- Planning a successful party

- Weaving attractive baskets (rugs, clothing, crafts)

- Building a house (boat, piece of furniture, and so on)

- Deciding on a career

- Hang gliding

- Riding a horse

- Playing chess (backgammon, chess, checkers, poker, and so on)

- Preventing accidents at home

- Traveling on a budget

- Applying to an American university

- Registering for classes

- Preparing to leave for your study abroad

WRITING EXERCISE

Write another essay telling your classmates how to do something that is unique to your culture. For example:

- Preparing a native dish

- Playing a musical instrument

- Crafting (weaving, pottery, garment, tool) something

- Dancing a native dance

- Playing a sport or game

- A cultural aspect that is different from what we do here in the United States

- Celebrating a holiday in your country

COMPARISON / CONTRAST ESSAYS

In your daily life you do a great deal of comparing and contrasting. When you show how much two or more things have in common, you compare. However, when you show how things are different, you contrast. In a supermarket you compare and contrast prices of brand-name and non-brand-name products, cuts of meat, and larger and smaller packages of food. In selecting a university, you look at the quality, location, cost, and variety of course offerings of each. When you think about living in an apartment or with a family, you analyze the advantages and the disadvantages of both. Through this process you arrive at your decisions. Convince other people of your opinion.

In order to write this type of essay effectively, it is necessary to narrow your focus. If you want, for example, to convince someone about the type of pet to buy, you will not try to compare and contrast five different animals and all their characteristics. It would be impossible to accomplish this adequately in a five-paragraph essay. Select, instead, at least three characteristics that you wish to emphasize for each pet compared. Obviously, after brainstorming you will have to eliminate all but what appear to be the most important to you. You should indicate to your readers the reason for selecting this method of comparison. Do not attempt to do both comparison and contrast in one essay. This would be very difficult and would result in a very long composition.

Make sure that you have two things that you can compare or contrast. If you wanted to contrast an ant and an elephant, where would you begin? One is an insect, and the other is a mammal. There is such a difference in the two that it would be almost impossible to write an effective essay.

Follow these suggestions for writing a good comparison or contrast essay.

Steps to Follow in Writing Comparison or Contrast Essays

* Narrow a broad topic so that you can focus on only three aspects instead of many.

* Be sure that the method you select is appropriate for your essay.

* Brainstorm thoroughly so that you can see both compare and contrast.

* Write a good outline before you begin to write the essay.

* Make your thesis statement specific so that readers know which method you have chosen.

* Begin your comparison essay by mentioning a few of the contrasts.

* Begin your contrast essay by mentioning a few of the comparisons.

* Use proper transitions so that your readers know what method you are developing.

* Compare or contrast by characteristic or by taking the elements as a whole.

* Write a conclusion that highlights the method you have chosen but also mentions the other method.

Comparison

Before you begin to write, select a topic that is not too broad. For example, if you wished to compare foreign students, select two students from the same country, two majoring in the same field, or two with the same lifestyle. If you are going to use colleges as your topic, narrow the topic to colleges that offer a particular program, two in the same city (state), or two that have similar or different histories.

In brainstorming the topic, write all the characteristics that come to mind, and then eliminate until you have the three most important ones that you plan to develop.

These transition words will carry you smoothly through your comparison essay:

in the same way	*similarly*	*just like*	*just as*
likewise	*in a like manner*	*by comparison*	

As you prepare to write your outline, keep in mind that there are two types that you can use. As you will see from the following diagrams, the easier of the two is to take one of the elements being compared and tell everything about it, and then go on to tell everything about the other. This type is called *comparing each as a whole*. For some reason, many writers find it easier to follow the other pattern. The second is *comparing by characteristics*. With this one, you will have a longer essay and outline. Neither is right or wrong. It just depends on your style of writing. Whichever style you choose will lead you to the same conclusion. Your final paragraph merely ties everything together, and it proves that you succeeded in doing what you had planned.

After brainstorming the topic and narrowing the essay's focus, one student wrote these two outlines for his essay, "Two Assassinated American Presidents."

By Characteristics

I. Introduction

    A. Thesis Statement

II. Northern Presidents and Southern Vice Presidents

    A. Abraham Lincoln

    B. John F. Kennedy

III. Human Rights

    A. Abraham Lincoln

    B. John F. Kennedy

IV. Assassination

    A. Abraham Lincoln

    B. John F. Kennedy

Conclusion

Each Element as a Whole

I. Introduction

    A. Thesis Statement

II. Abraham Lincoln

    A. Northern President, Southern Vice President

    B. Human Rights

    C. Assassination

III. John F. Kennedy

    A. Northern President, Southern Vice President

    B. Human Rights

    C. Assassination

Conclusion

If you are writing a comparison essay, start your introduction paragraph by indicating several contrasts between the items you will compare. Then use sentences with transition words such as *however*, *despite*, and *even though* to show that you are not planning to contrast but rather to compare. After that, list the three or more elements that you will use for your comparison in your thesis statement.

DISCUSSION EXERCISE:

The following essay, "Two Assassinated American Presidents," compares by characteristic two American presidents who were assassinated. Before you read the essay, discuss the following questions.

1. Why were Abraham Lincoln and John F. Kennedy great men?

2. Who in your country's history has also been considered great?

3. Were these people in your country political leaders?

4. When did they live?

5. What does "assassination" mean?

6. What other important people have been assassinated throughout the centuries?

7. After you have read this essay, discuss the significance of the similarities in these men's lives.

Purpose:	to emphasize the similarities in the lives of two great American presidents
Audience:	instructor, other students, history majors
Method:	Comparison by characteristics
Thesis Statement:	Despite the differences in their lives, their presidential terms had a surprising number of similarities: Northern-reared presidents with Southern vice presidents, attempts to pacify growing national discontent, assassinations, and the succession of their vice presidents.

Two Assassinated American Presidents

Abraham Lincoln and John F. Kennedy were two very popular American presidents. Their personal lives were rather different. Lincoln came from a poor family and learned to read and write at home, mostly by candlelight. Kennedy's family was very wealthy and sent him to the best schools in the East. Lincoln eventually became a lawyer, and although Kennedy reluctantly studied law, he preferred a career as a writer. Despite the differences in their lives, their presidential terms had a surprising number of similarities: Northern-reared presidents with southern vice presidents, attempts to pacify growing national discontent, assassinations, and the succession of their vice presidents.

Both presidents were reared in Northern states. Despite his birth in Kentucky, Abraham Lincoln lived most of his life in Springfield, Illinois, while John Kennedy was born in and lived most of his life in Brookline, Massachusetts.

Strangely enough, both vice presidents were Southern born, and were selected as running mates in an attempt to pacify the country politically. Lincoln's vice president, Andrew Johnson, was born in Raleigh, North Carolina, in 1808. Exactly 100 years later Kennedy's vice president, Lyndon B. Johnson, was born in Johnson City, Texas.

Both focused their presidencies on human rights issues. Lincoln fought for the elimination of slavery throughout the Union, especially in the South. Kennedy was most outspoken about civil rights and more freedom for blacks, especially in Southern states. Both were greatly loved by the great majority of Americans.

Both men perpetuated the dubious tradition of those presidents elected in years ending in zero who have died in office. On the fateful assassination days, both men were seated, enjoying the events of the moment. Lincoln and his wife were attending the performance of a comedy at Ford's Theater in Washington when a Southern sympathizer entered his theater box and shot him in the back of the head. Likewise, John Kennedy was shot in the back of the head as he rode in an open-top car with his wife as the two waved cheerfully to the well-wishers watching the parade along the streets of Dallas, Texas.

Despite the differences in their lives, Abraham Lincoln and John F. Kennedy will be remembered for their greatness as presidents, their concern for human rights, and the violent deaths that fate had in store for them.

VOCABULARY EXPANSION

wealthy – very rich

reluctantly – unwillingly

reared – brought to maturity

pacify – to bring peace

running mate – usually the candidate for vice president

outspoken – open in speech

perpetuated – continued forever

presidency – presidential term in office

Following the outline for the previous essay, another student wrote an essay taking each element as a whole. He used the same introductory and conclusion paragraphs as the first student but created different developmental paragraphs. In paragraph 2, he describes events and circumstances unique to Lincoln's presidency. He talks about the president's origins, as well as those of his vice president, the focus of his presidency, and the circumstances and events surrounding his assassination. Paragraph 3 highlights similar aspects of John F. Kennedy's presidency and background and notes how they parallel those of Lincoln. Notice how the writer presents facts in these two paragraphs. Pay particular attention to the transition words he uses in comparing the two.

Purpose:	to emphasize the similarities in the lives of two great American presidents
Audience:	instructor, other students, history majors
Method:	Comparison, each element as a whole
Thesis Statement:	Despite the differences in their lives, their presidential terms had a surprising number of similarities: Northern-reared presidents with Southern vice presidents, attempts to pacify growing national discontent, assassinations, and the succession of their vice presidents.

Two Assassinated American Presidents

Abraham Lincoln and John F. Kennedy were two very popular American presidents. Their personal lives were rather different. Lincoln came from a poor family and learned to read and write at home, mostly by candlelight. Kennedy's family was very wealthy and sent him to the best schools in the East. Lincoln eventually became a lawyer, and although Kennedy reluctantly studied law, he preferred a career as a writer. Despite the differences in their lives, their presidential terms had a surprising number of similarities: Northern-reared presidents with Southern vice presidents, attempts to pacify growing national discontent, assassinations, and the succession of their vice presidents.

Abraham Lincoln, despite his birth in Kentucky, lived all of his life in Springfield, Illinois. His vice president, Andrew Johnson, however, was born in Raleigh, North Carolina, in 1808. Lincoln chose Johnson as the running mate in an attempt to unify the country politically during his term in office. Lincoln fought for human rights and for the elimination of slavery throughout the Union, especially in the South. The majority of Americans loved him very much. Lincoln was the second president (William Henry Harrison, elected in 1840, was the first) elected in a year ending in zero to die in office. He and his wife were attending the performance of a comedy at Ford's Theatre in Washington when a Southern sympathizer entered his theater box and shot the president in the back of the head.

John F. Kennedy's life contains many of the same characteristics as that of Lincoln. The former was born and lived most of his life in Brookline, Massachusetts. He also chose a Southern running mate, hoping to unify a politically divided country in the 1960s. Lyndon B. Johnson, strangely enough, had the same last name as Lincoln's vice president and was born exactly 100 years after Andrew Johnson. Kennedy was also greatly loved by the American public. He spoke out for civil rights and more freedom for blacks, especially in Southern states. Like Lincoln, he, too, continued the dubious tradition of dying in office. He was the seventh president elected in a year ending in zero to die while serving his term. Similar to Lincoln's assassination, Kennedy and his wife were seated in an open-top car, waving cheerfully to the well-wishers watching the parade along the streets of Dallas, Texas. His assailant also shot him in the back of the head.

Despite the differences in their lives, the world will remember Abraham Lincoln and John F. Kennedy for their greatness as presidents, their concern for human rights, and the violent deaths that fate had in store for them.

Read the essay "Two Great American Cities" and then follow the instructions in the writing exercise.

Purpose:	to show that despite their great cultural differences, New York City and Cleveland, Ohio, have many things in common
Audience:	instructor, other students, tourists
Method:	Comparison by characteristics
Thesis Statement:	Although New York City and Cleveland, Ohio, seem to be quite different, they are similar in many ways: location, climate, and entertainment.

Two Great American Cities

New York City and Cleveland, Ohio, are two very different cities. New York has a population more than seven times as great as that of Cleveland. The former has a greater cultural variety because more ethnic groups choose to live and work there. While there is a high crime rate in Cleveland, the city does not experience the large number of violent crimes as does the "Big Apple," as New York City is sometimes called. Although New York City and Cleveland seem to be quite different, they are similar in many ways: location, climate, and entertainment.

Both cities are located on major shipping routes. New York City sees the arrival and departure of numerous ocean-going vessels every day. Much of the nation's supply of goods passes through its ports every 24 hours. Cleveland is home to a large volume of the Great Lakes' shipping along the St. Lawrence River, some of which makes its way to international waters.

Climate in both cities is very similar. As New York is subjected to harsh, Arctic winds and deep, snowy winters, so is Cleveland. Temperatures often plummet below zero and remain there for many days. Pedestrians and motorists are often stranded as strong winds and driving snowstorms fiercely attack those who venture far from home.

Entertainment plays a major role in the lives of the citizens of both cities. Many museums, large and small, abound in New York; visitors flock to the Metropolitan Museum, the Guggenheim, and other famous galleries. The Cleveland Art Museum is renowned for its famous art collections and was once among a select few to display Egyptian treasures. The New York Philharmonic Orchestra and the Cleveland Symphony Orchestra are world famous for their concerts and other musical presentations.

Despite the differences in culture, population, and the number of crimes, New York City and Cleveland, Ohio, have a great deal in common. Both great cities portray many similarities in their importance in shipping, their climate, and a variety of entertainment. They are two wonderful cities.

VOCABULARY EXPANSION

ocean-going vessels – ships that travel on the high seas

subjected – be under the control of another

harsh – cruel, bitter

plummet – to drop rapidly

pedestrians – people on foot

stranded – can't leave an area because of difficulty

flock – (v.) to gather in large numbers

portray – to display, show

fiercely – strongly

venture – to wander, travel

galleries – places for exhibits, especially for art exhibits

WRITING EXERCISE

Work as a group to do the following exercise. Using the presidential essay as a model, rewrite the previous article on the two cities. Describe each entity as a whole. Repeat the introduction and conclusion paragraphs, but change the body to include only two paragraphs. Prepare an outline to guide your writing.

WRITING EXERCISE

Select two of the following topics and write a 250-word essay on each. Be sure to brainstorm carefully and begin your essay by contrasting some of the elements. Then lead into the similarities of each. Provide as many details as possible to create a well-developed essay. You may use either method for your development.

- Compare two fast food restaurants. Even though they serve different food, show similarities in quality, service, cleanliness, friendliness, cost, nutritional value of the food, and so on.

- Compare two people who on the surface seem different but who are really very similar: personality, ideals, major area of study, and so on.

- Compare two authors in the same or different fields: content, appeal, techniques, and so on.

- Compare two musicians (solos or groups): types of music, style, appeal, dress, and so on.

- Compare two languages: vocabulary, grammar, sounds (pronunciation).

- Compare two countries: government, population, economy, religion.

- Compare two cities: your hometown and the city where you currently live.

- Compare two university systems: universities in your country and those in the United States.

Contrast

This type of essay emphasizes differences when comparing. The introductory paragraph begins by stating how the two elements compared are similar. Then the reader is informed that the essay will actually discuss the differences between the two. Always mention in the introductory paragraph the elements that you have chosen to contrast. If you choose to contrast by characteristics, each of the developmental paragraphs will discuss only one element of contrast between the two. In the conclusion you might briefly mention again the similarities, but the overall emphasis here too should be on differences. You can apply the same format as you did for the comparison essay.

Your choice of transition words is very important. Make sure that they show a contrast. In the following essays the ones most frequently used are *on the other hand, however, except for,* and *while*. Besides transition words, you can use adjectives that end in _er_ or _est_ or use *more* or *most* plus the adjective (more economical, higher priced, worse, better, etc.)

In each of the developmental paragraphs, start with a general statement (your topic sentence) and move to the specific by providing as many details as you can. Examine carefully the outlines below and how one group of students approached writing an essay on a sports-related topic. Did they leave out any important information?

Americans practice many kinds of sports today. Sports as a general category is much too broad a topic to write about. Narrow it down to two particular sports, such as football and baseball. What are some of the ideas that come from brainstorming?

BRAINSTORMING FOR FOOTBALL AND BASEBALL

Similarities

popularity

played on artificial turf or grass

require special equipment

professional and non-professional leagues

Differences

equipment—head gear, uniforms, shoes	seasons
number of players on field	football is played in rain or snow
baseball isn't played in rain or snow	contact or non-contact sport
players' salaries	physical size of players

Although there are similarities between the two sports, you can see through brainstorming that the most important characteristics are found in the differences category. You will need to eliminate some of them, but clearly with so many significant differences, you will be able to write a better contrast than comparison essay. Unless you are writing a term paper, you will not need to write on all of the differences you listed.

Here are two outlines the students produced, illustrating the two methods for comparing or contrasting. Notice that the first is longer. Both contain the same information, but the first has one extra paragraph. This group of students chose to contrast by characteristics and followed the first outline. Notice that they mentioned some similarities in the introductory paragraph but indicated in their thesis statements that they were planning to discuss the differences.

Contrasting by characteristics

Par. I Introduction
      Topic Sentence:
Par. II Equipment
      A. Football
      B. Baseball
Par. III Structure of the games
      A. Football
      B. Baseball
Par. IV. Playing Fields
      A. Football
      B. Baseball
Conclusion

Contrasting each element as a whole

Par. I. Introduction

         Topic Sentence:

Par. II. Football

        A. Equipment

        B. Structure of the game

        C. Playing fields

Par. III. Baseball

        A. Equipment

        B. Structure of the game

        C. Playing fields

Conclusion

Purpose:	to show the major differences which exist between football and baseball
Audience:	instructor; other students; athletes
Method:	contrast by characteristics
Thesis Statement:	The major differences are the protective equipment, game structure, and field design

Two Popular American Sports

Baseball and football are two American sports that many people enjoy. Although the two games are similar in popularity, turf, and league organization, they are different in many ways. The major differences are in the protective equipment, game structure, and field design.

Both sets of players require different attire. Since football is a full-contact sport, players wear heavy equipment, which is not necessary for baseball players. Football headgear consists of a well-padded helmet made of impact-resistant plastic. It has a face guard and chin strap. However, baseball players wear a cap that has only a bill in the front to shade the player's eyes from the sun. Batters wear a small plastic hat to protect themselves against wild pitches from the pitcher. Except for the catcher, baseball players wear no upper-body protection, while football players wear heavy shoulder pads covered by a loose jersey. Football pants are also well-padded in the knees, thighs, and hips. Baseball pants, on the other hand, offer no protection. Shoes are basically the same except that baseball players wear metal spikes instead of rubber ones.

The structure of the games is very different. Football consists of two halves divided equally into two fifteen-minute quarters, which usually last longer than the actual set time because the clock stops and starts with each play. On the other hand, a baseball game is divided into nine or more innings. Each has six outs, three per team. The innings last as long as it takes for both teams to get three outs. In case of a tie at the end of nine innings, teams continue to play until one of the teams breaks the tie. Sometimes, depending on the level of the league, there are tie-breakers in football also.

The playing fields are geometrically different also. The football field is one hundred yards long, is rectangular, and is divided into ten-yard sections. At each end there is a touchdown zone and a goal post. The baseball field is diamond shaped, and the middle section, or infield, contains four bases and a pitcher's mound. In the surrounding area called the outfield, three players try to catch any long-distance hits. Two dugouts, one for each team, provide teammates a place to wait their turn to play.

Despite their similarities in popularity, the type of turf, and the leagues, both American sports differ significantly in the equipment used, the structure of the game, and the field design.

VOCABULARY EXPANSION

turf – grassy surface

attire – dress, costume

headgear – hat

bill – rim of a hat, usually used to protect one's eyes from the sun

jersey – long shirt

spikes – sharp-pointed pieces of metal on the bottom of the shoes

tie – when both teams have the same score

mound – an artificial elevation of land

padded – having some soft cushion of comfort or protection

pitch – (v.) to throw the ball to the batter

pitcher – the player who throws the ball to the batter

catcher – the player who is behind the batter at home plate who receives the ball thrown by the pitcher

innings – segments of a baseball game; each inning sees each team at bat once

touchdown – when players put the football in their end zone and score six points

dugout – covered area for players to stay when they are not at bat or on the field in baseball

WRITING EXERCISE

Following the outline pattern for contrasting elements as a whole, write an essay on football and baseball, using the information provided above.

In this short essay, the writer shows how it is possible to contrast two foreign students. Notice how the writer narrowed the topic to the personalities of two German students. Read how he brainstormed the topic below, and then read the essay that resulted from it.

BRAINSTORMING FOR FOREIGN STUDENTS

Hans

went to St. Michael High School   23 years old

lives alone   drives a Mazda

outgoing, lazy   gets C's and D's

macho   lifts weights

has many girlfriends   spends time developing his tan

goes to parties and discos every night   goal: work on his father's horse ranch

Klaus

went to St. Michael High School   23 years old

has roommates   rides a bike

timid   hard working, gets A's and B's

down-to-earth, athletic   has one girlfriend

spends quiet evenings studying with girlfriend   spends time in the library

goal: become an expert on international law

Two Students from Germany

Although both Hans and Klaus are the same age and attended the same high school in their native Germany, their personalities and lifestyles are quite different. Hans is a lazy, fun-loving person who enjoys having beautiful women around him. He has many girlfriends and spends all of his free time working out with his weights and developing his tan at the beach or around the pool of his apartment complex. Every night he goes to parties and dances in the local discotheques. Consequently, Hans does not have much time to study. His lack of dedication is obvious, since his grades are not very high. Hans's father is wealthy and owns a horse-breeding farm and hopes that his son will help him run it someday. At the moment, Hans does not want to think of having any responsibilities. His present goal is to have fun and enjoy life.

Klaus, on the other hand, is timid, hardworking, and studious. He has only one girlfriend, and they usually spend their evenings studying in the library, jogging, or bicycle riding. His dedication results in good grades in school. His hard work is preparing him for a wonderful career and a great future. Klaus hopes to become an expert on international law and is working hard to achieve that goal. His extra hours spent in the law library are preparing him for law school.

While Hans and Klaus are two students who lead similar lives, their activities and goals are very different. Klaus is a high academic achiever, while Hans prefers to be more sociable and fun loving.

Another group of students chose to contrast two old cars. They also selected the method of contrast by characteristics. After they had finished brainstorming, eliminating, and outlining, they began to write their essay. However, they did not have enough time to finish. Working from their brainstorming, finish the essay. The topic sentence for paragraphs 3 and 4 are already written for you. Provide many supporting details and a good conclusion.

Check out the Internet for more information regarding performance and fuel economy to help yourself finish the two paragraphs.

BRAINSTORMING

(information acquired from owners' manuals for both cars)

1990 BMW (Austrian)

160 mph approx.	low-fuel warning lights
12-20 mpg	leather and velour interior
193.3" length	rear-window defogger
6- or 12-cylinder	on-board computerized system
21.4-gal. tank	dependability
5-speed manual transmission	maintenance
automatic fuel and oil indicators	style
cellular telephone	materials
anti-theft radio and air bags are standard	details
memory seat and mirror position	

1985 Nissan Sentra (Japanese)

105 mph maximum	cloth and vinyl interior
28-44 mpg	child restraints
166.9" length	dependable racing city or country roads
4-cylinder	mileage
13.25-gal. tank	Japan
4- or 5-speed	style
automatic fuel and oil indicators	materials
car phone not standard equipment	details
low-fuel warning lights	

The BMW and the Nissan

BMW and Nissan are two makes of cars that many people test-drive. Although the two makes of cars are similar in their capabilities and service, they are different in many ways. The main differences are in their appearance, performance, and fuel economy.

Both makes of cars appear to be attractive from different perspectives. However, the BMW is superior in detail, design, and technology. It has more attractive lines, leather and plush interior, airbags, double-lock doors and trunks, cellular telephone, and an anti-theft radio as standard equipment. Nissan meets the standards as well as the price range of the average American; therefore, it consists of mostly cheaper plastics, rubber compounds, and metals, which greatly reduce the price. The BMW also is made from some of these materials, but the Bavarian sports car professionals who designed this car put it together with infinite care in order to obtain the utmost in quality and performance for a costly automobile such as this.

Performance is also a contributing factor, which may deter some in deciding on which new car to purchase. The BMW, as well as the Nissan, is both dependable and virtually maintenance free. _____

_____

_____

_____

_____

Fuel economy is one of the most distinguishing characteristics of these two automobiles. _____

_____

_____

_____

_____

In brief _____

_____

_____

_____

_____

> ## WRITING EXERCISE
>
> Select one of the following topics and write a paper contrasting the elements mentioned. Set up an outline to guide you as you write.

- Leisure Activities in the United States and in Your Country

- Food and Nutrition in the United States and in Your Country

- Two Teachers

- Two Sports You Have Played

- Two Tourist Attractions

- Two Museums You Have Visited

- Two Careers

- Holidays in Your Country or Holidays in the United States

- Family Life in the United States and in Your Country

PERSUASION ESSAYS

In a persuasion essay, writers must convince readers of their point of view. The best way to argue convincingly in a paper is to take a definite stand and then provide as many supporting details as you can. When writers take a stand, they should think of themselves as political candidates who are out campaigning and trying to convince people to vote for them. They should express ideas that will catch their listeners' attention and persuade them that they are the best of all the candidates.

If writers do not take a firm positive or negative stand on the issue, they will never convince the readers. They should state only what they know to be facts. Many persuasion papers use statistics to support the writers' point of view. This will mean doing some research in the library and providing a list of sources of available information so that readers can follow up on the data if they so choose.

Would the following supporting details be acceptable to include in a persuasion paper? Do they represent quotes or statistics from reliable sources?

Example A: The Environmental Protection Agency reports that air in the country is purer than that in the city, thus making the former a better place to live. *to them, therefore*

(The EPA is a highly reliable government source, so the data should be reliable.)

Example B: Analyses from reports by Educational Testing Service prove that higher SAT scores are due, in part, to the study of foreign languages.

(ETS has a strong record for accuracy and reliability.)

Example C: Veteran sportscaster Bob Russell says that Rick Davis of the Campton Cougars holds the record for the most strikeouts in a baseball game.

(Bob Russell should be an expert on baseball, since he has been broadcasting the game for many years.)

Example D: My sister, who is in the third grade, says that all of the fourth-grade boys are stupid.

(She has no experience in the fourth grade, so her information would not be very reliable.)

Steps to Follow in Writing Persuasion Essays

- Select a topic you know very well.

- Strive for a catchy beginning.

- Get your readers' attention and hold it.

- Brainstorm or make a list of ideas to support your point of view.

- Let your readers know your point of view in the thesis statement.

- Use expressions like should (not), ought (not) to, must (not), fair, unfair, better, worse.

- Develop from the general to the specific.

- Be honest, convincing, and not too general.

- Quote authorities and use reliable statistics.

- Save your best argument for last.

- Write a good conclusion that emphasizes your viewpoint.

In each of the following essays, decide whether the authors clearly state their point of view. Are they convincing? What is the thesis statement? Are there enough supporting details to convince you? Which one of them is the most convincing? Does the conclusion restate the writer's point of view?

Return to the 55-mph Speed Limit

When people travel in the twenty-first century, they are in a hurry to arrive at their destination. On the highways they exceed the limits, which can be costly in terms of lives and dollars. The government should return to the 55-mph speed limit in the United States to prevent so many highway fatalities and to lower the high consumption of gasoline.

Accidents kill thousands of people on our highways and expressways every year. Most accidents are the result of reckless driving at excessive speeds. Drivers could avoid such needless slaughter if they obeyed the limits. The state government needs to provide more highway patrolmen to monitor speeds and apprehend those exceeding the limits. The revenues generated by the high fines would pay the salaries of the additional workforce. Violators would learn, if only in a negative sense, the importance of obeying the laws.

As the world's supply of fuel becomes more and more uncertain every day, the need for thriftiness becomes more evident. Gasoline prices have risen to unprecedented heights in the last four years, and although there has been some fluctuation, the lower prices have never been long lasting. Traveling at speeds greater than 55 mph causes cars to consume larger quantities of gasoline, thus increasing the cost of travel to the consumer and a greater demand for gasoline.

In order to prevent high death tolls on our highways and to reduce the excessive consumption of gasoline by fast-traveling vehicles, the government must reenact the 55-mph speed limit on our highways. If not, current speed limits will be extremely costly in terms of natural resources and, importantly, human lives.

VOCABULARY EXPANSION

exceed – to surpass, go beyond

excessive – passing the limit; going beyond the limit

reckless – not careful

needless – unnecessary

slaughter – killing

apprehend – to stop

thriftiness – being careful with money

unprecedented – never happened before

fluctuation – going up and down

death toll – the number of dead

Drug Problems

A growing number of drug pushers, users, and motorists under the influence of drugs and alcohol are endangering lives of unsuspecting victims. The United States has neither a strong control over nor a consistent enforcement against drugs. If this country is to be an example to the rest of the world, our law enforcement agencies, educational institutions, and automobile associations must unite in an all-out campaign to see that everyone, especially young people, becomes more aware of the dangers to their health, livelihood, and general well-being. Everyone must strive to eliminate violent drug-related crimes and accidents.

State officials must pass laws imposing high fines and other penalties for drug pushers and users. After finding the accused guilty, courts should order execution for those who peddle drugs in schools, especially elementary and high schools. When the police catch addicts or others possessing drugs or paraphernalia, the former should impose large fines on the guilty parties and imprison them with no possibility for parole. This will impress upon these people the threat that they are to the community. Mexico, Turkey, and other countries severely punish offenders. The United States must do the same.

Schools should offer special programs. Teachers must inform students of the effects of drugs on the brain, as well as on the nervous and reproductive systems. Taking drugs can damage body functions and possibly produce abnormal future generations. These future citizens will become a tremendous burden on society, a society that cannot presently meet the needs of its mentally retarded and physically handicapped.

Automobile associations should work with the police department to provide films and literature that focuses on accidents that have occurred as a result of the drivers' being under the influence of drugs and alcohol. Seeing real-life dramas and their consequences should persuade youth to avoid any form of narcotic. Insurance companies can also provide incentives by giving lower rates to motorists who do not use drugs and by canceling policies when their clients have drug-related accidents. The state government can also punish these offenders by revoking driving privileges and confiscating their cars.

If our country puts forth an all-out effort to curtail drug use, the people here will live in a safer environment. Its citizens will not have to worry about brutal crimes and horrible highway accidents. If the United States is to survive, the government must enforce stronger laws against drug pushers, users, and motorists under the influence of drugs and alcohol.

VOCABULARY EXPANSION

consistent – always the same

all-out – total, complete

livelihood – way of living

imposing – levying, charging

paraphernalia – accessories, equipment

tremendous – great

retarded – delayed development

incentives – motives, stimuli (plural of stimulus)

revoking – canceling, taking away (as in taking away a license, certificate)

confiscating – taking away some property, personal belongings

curtail – to stop, cut short

incur – to bring about

campaign – a series of operations undertaken to meet a specific goal

drug pusher – one who sells narcotics

peddle – to sell drugs illegally

addicts – persons unable to control desire for and use of certain substances

parole – early release of prisoners based on their good behavior

narcotic – drug such as heroin, morphine, and cocaine that becomes addictive with prolonged use

Esperanto

As we move into the twenty-first century, the need for a universal language becomes more and more apparent. Tourism increases by greater numbers every year as people become far more mobile than ever before. Satellite broadcasts can be seen simultaneously throughout the world. Commercial ventures unite the four corners of the universe and bring many products within reach of the average consumer with instructions for use or assembly in several languages. There are a greater number of scientific and technological exchanges at international conferences than ever before. As we become more mobile, we also move our residences with greater ease. With so much interaction, a universal language would eliminate so many problems of misunderstanding in business and communication.

Hundreds of types of artificial languages have been developed using forms of existing words, combinations of numbers, and a series of pictures. Most were unsuccessful because of complicated structures and/or pronunciation. Some appealed only to a more scholarly audience.

How would linguists organize the ideal language? First and foremost, they should create one that would appeal to all levels of society in a logical and uncomplicated format. Pronunciation should be simplified with the use of one sound per letter. Letters or symbols must be easily recognizable. The language should be flexible with the right amount of vocabulary to facilitate communication effectively in a variety of areas. Most important, it should be easy and quick to learn.

English is not an appropriate model because there are too many rules and exceptions that frustrate learners. The pronunciation and spelling are difficult because each letter can have several possible sounds. Two words can be spelled the same way and have different pronunciation and meaning. Another set of words could be spelled differently and have the same pronunciation but different meanings. There are too many irregular verbs, which follow no organized patterns, as well as an abundance of tenses and grammatical moods. English sentence structure is also complicated and often frustrating for the new learner.

Esperanto, meaning "one who hopes," has been the most popular and long-lasting artificial language since its development in 1897. It has a simple structure based on a 28-letter alphabet with only 16 grammar rules. It has been modified a number of times since its creation and has acquired worldwide acceptance as an international means of communication. Many universities offer it as a regular foreign language, and many international scientific conferences use it as the spoken language. Many people throughout the world read a number of scholarly magazines and journals written in Esperanto. Because of its universal acceptance, uncomplicated grammar, simplified pronunciation, and ease of communication, Esperanto should be the universal language of the future.

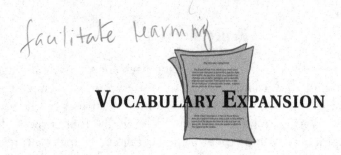

VOCABULARY EXPANSION

apparent – visible, easily seen

mobile – able to move or be moved from one place to another

ventures – dangerous endeavors or ones whose outcome is uncertain

simultaneously – happening at the same time

linguists – specialists in languages or persons who speak several languages

foremost – ahead of all others

format – produced in a certain form

frustrate – to keep someone from fulfilling his desires

scholarly – showing much intellectual learning

WRITING EXERCISE

The following is a paired assignment. With a partner, select one of the following topics and write a persuasion essay of approximately 300 words. Remember to take a definite point of view either in favor of or against the issue. Most of all, be convincing.

WRITING EXERCISE

The following is an individual assignment. Select a different topic and write a persuasion essay of approximately 300 words. Remember to take a definite point of view either in favor of or against the issue. Most of all, be convincing.

- The need for using safety belts while driving

- Welfare systems must be closely monitored

- The death penalty should (not) be abolished

- The need to protect our natural resources

- Partial-birth abortions as a means of birth control must (not) be banned in the United States

- The government should (not) ban the manufacture and use of nuclear weapons

- Separate areas in public places should (not) be provided for non-smokers

- Gun control should (not) be mandated by law

- The government should (not) legalize the use of marijuana for medicinal purposes

- A college education is (not) necessary for finding a good job

- Voters should (not) elect a president for a maximum six-year term in office

- Hitchhiking is dangerous and should be punishable by law

- Homosexual marriage should (not) be legalized

- The Kyoto Agreement should (not) be recognized by the United States

- The Nuclear Nonproliferation Treaty should (not) be strictly enforced by the United Nations

- University students have to be fluent in a second language in order to qualify for graduation

- The United States should (not) withdraw from the United Nations

- The United States and other developed countries should (not) increase foreign aid to developing nations

REACTION ESSAYS

Life in the twentieth and twenty-first centuries has presented us with numerous situations that we have never encountered, nor did we expect them to affect their lives so strongly. How people react to these situations depends on their level of involvement and their background. Students often find many situations to which they must react in either a social or an academic setting. For the latter, they often have assignments for classes that will force them to write their reaction to a test question or something that they have read. In the former, the instructor has presented all the material on a particular subject and on a test expects the students to assimilate all that they have learned and to react to a given situation. In music, art, or drama appreciation classes, it is often necessary for students to attend a number of functions and write a critique of them. A spring or fall arts festival can generate material for a lengthy essay. Students are forced to express their opinions and must provide numerous details to defend their thesis. They could also find themselves at a loss for words when they have no opinion on the subject.

In literature classes, students may have to react to a story they have just read. Sometimes the central idea is revolting to them, and they would prefer not to discuss the matter. In the short story "A Rose for Emily," by William Faulkner, the central character kills her male friend because he will not marry her. She then keeps the man's body in bed with her. Quite some time later members of the community insist on entering the house and find the skeletal remains of the man. What if students were reading this story and their instructor asked them to comment on it? They would have to express their opinions and provide details to support them, or they could willingly express how satisfied the story made them feel.

In world history classes instructors might ask students to react to Alexander the Great's, Napoleon's, or Adolf Hitler's ideas of conquering the world; the Spanish Inquisition; explorations in the New World; or the American civil rights movement. Students would have to read a great deal on these topics to be able to come up with a viable response to them. There is no definite right nor wrong answer, just whatever they feel about the situation.

An effective persuasion essay expresses a definite opinion. Writers cannot take a middle-of-the-road stance. Some writers can become so infuriated by a situation that they lose sight of reality, and they overstate or misinterpret facts and relay false information to their audience. They must be objective in their reactions, and plan their essay well.

Steps to Follow in Writing Reaction Essays

- Pay closer attention to class lectures when you know that you will be writing an essay for part of the exam.

- Read the material several times to ensure that you did not misinterpret what you read.

- Don't overreact to what you have heard or read.

- Take a firm stand.

- Focus on the issue itself and not on a number of unrelated events.

- Be sure to compose an outline and respond carefully to each point that you write.

- Be objective and do not stereotype.

- Plan carefully your brainstorming and outlining.

- Present your point of view clearly.

- Let your readers know in the first paragraph exactly how you feel about the situation.

DISCUSSION EXERCISE

Read the following essay, which reacts to a television presentation on the recovery of the artifacts of the *Titanic*.

1) Did the writer overreact to the issue?

2) What is the thesis statement?

3) What supporting details did he/she provide to support the opinion expressed?

4) Were the comparisons valid in their relation to the main issue?

5) How would you react to the same situation?

Background information:

In the spring of 1988 a television special presented the story of the ill-fated luxury liner *Titanic*, which sank during the ship's first voyage after hitting an iceberg. Since 1914 the ship, its contents, and over one thousand people have lain in an icy grave thousands of feet below the surface of the North Sea. Several organizations have recently tried to bring up the artifacts and display them in a museum so that others could see them. On this particular program, the presenters showed a few of the artifacts found that were of relatively little importance. A gigantic debate ensued, in which the pros and cons of disturbing the dead and the untouched grave of more than ninety years ago were argued. One group proposed displaying as many artifacts as could be recovered and then inviting the public to see them. The other group vehemently opposed such an idea. Lengthy debates were part of the weekly programming that followed. The following essay is the reaction of one writer who favored exhibiting the artifacts.

Exhibiting the *Titanic*'s Artifacts

The recent *Titanic* presentation with Telly Savalas as narrator left a great deal to be desired. A debate on the television program *Crossfire* on whether to retrieve artifacts from the deep and display them in museums was even more upsetting. The recovered artifacts are an integral part of history, especially for Americans. The best way to preserve this history is through an educational public exhibit. Because this event affected people worldwide, the artifacts should be part of a traveling exhibit.

None of us lived during the War Between the States, but we can learn a great deal about the period through battle reenactments and museum presentations. Tallahassee, Florida's exhibit of the *Mary Rose* in 1987 gave a great deal of insight into man's folly as well as providing a link to centuries past. Henry VIII's military advisers suggested covering the warship *Mary Rose* with a special netting so that the French could not board and attack the sailors. The theory was good, but on the day that the newly refurbished ship set sail from the harbor, it was overloaded with men and cargo and sank at the foot of the well-wishers on the docks. The enemy-proof netting had trapped the sailors within, killing most of them. The museum's exhibit of a model and sketches of the ship made this aspect of history far more vivid than reading about it in a textbook. Surely an exhibit on the *Titanic* would allow mankind to benefit from the foolishness of others.

In 1986 Mel Fisher's son gave a slide lecture at a local university. Prior to the presentation, I had an opportunity to speak with him. When he found out that I was an amateur historian and a Spanish instructor, he handed me a gold bar from the *Atocha* (a seventeenth-century Spanish galleon that sank off the coast of Florida) and proceeded to explain all of its markings. This was an extremely emotional moment for me to hold three hundred years of history and $50,000 in my hand! An opportunity like that will never come my way again. Later during the presentation a young woman commented on how she had visited the Fisher Treasure Museum in the Florida Keys, and had it not been for Mel's interest in sharing those artifacts, she and many others would never have gotten to explore firsthand this fascinating period of history. The Fishers had donated a number of objects to the Florida government, but today they lie hidden in a vault in Tallahassee.

Museums are meant to display history and to help people relive it. The *Titanic* adventure is one that should be shared with everyone. Exhibiting the artifacts from the sunken ship in public places and displaying photos of the people who died so tragically on the *Titanic* should be welcomed, not discouraged.

VOCABULARY EXPANSION

artifacts – manmade objects

reenactments – live performance of a past activity

folly – stupidity, foolishness

refurbished – renovated

trapped – unable to escape

surely – certainly

galleon – a large Spanish ship used during the Colonial period

Telly Savalas – bald American actor of Greek origin noted for his television role as Lt. Theo Kojak

integral – complete, whole

sketches – drawings

amateur – not professional

vault – strongbox for storing valuables

The following appeared in a local newspaper as a reaction to an article about an area resident who was earning a great deal of money as a distributor of pornographic literature. Consider the following questions as you read.

1) Did the writer overreact to the issue?

2) What is the thesis statement?

3) What supporting details did he/she provide to support the opinion expressed?

4) Were the comparisons valid in their relation to the main issue?

5) How would you react to the same situation?

Local Porn King Makes Big

Journalism in our area reached an all-time low today, when our local newspaper published an article on the front page dealing with the city's X-rated connection and praised John Doe as the California dream machine. Mr. Doe, a young, wealthy porn movie mogul, promotes young sexy women who "embody girl-next-door wholesomeness." For your information, women who engage in "multiple sex, nude dancing, breast implants, and monthly disease tests" do *not* embody wholesomeness. This article on the front page, no less, promotes an immoral element of society that, in part, contributes to the degeneration of society. Your paper praises a man who has profited from the pornographic trade and whose father served as a lieutenant to a former porn czar. Where is your sense of values in promoting this garbage on the front page of a family newspaper?

On the other hand, buried in the very last section of the paper is a wonderful article about the "Teacher of the Year," someone who has sacrificed a great deal and done so much for the youth of this state, the future leaders of tomorrow. The latter will read your article and feel that they are wasting their time on the basics of math, reading, science, English, and social studies. They will think that it is easier and more fun to earn lots of money doing something less academically productive. Their families are struggling to survive. They see that and decide that pornography is a better way to survive in a better lifestyle. Mr. Doe helps promote promiscuous young women, while the teacher is trying to help students make a better life for themselves. The teacher helps them get dignified jobs so that they can make valuable contributions to society and be in touch with the real world.

Your newspaper has to reevaluate its sense of values and print the news that is fit to print, the news that glorifies the real heroes of society and not the smut peddlers, the dregs of humanity who make a fast buck selling their garbage. I'm canceling my subscription because of your less-than-professional journalism.

VOCABULARY EXPANSION

beleaguered – surrounded by problems with no escape from them

dream machine – person responsible for prosperity and bringing about happy times

mogul – powerful and important person

embody – to represent

wholesomeness – promoting healthy lifestyle

degeneration – to fall apart

czar – king or promoter

promiscuous – having casual, sexual relations often with different people

smut peddlers – those who sell/deliver pornographic materials

dregs of humanity – worthless people

fast buck – make quick money

X-rated – code of regulations indicating unacceptable because of violence, nudity, language, and so on

porn – short form of pornography that deals with explicit sex and nudity

salutes – praises

lieutenant – a rank of police officer

sacrificed – gave up certain things or practices for the betterment of self or others

Ireneo Funes

Jorge Luis Borges, a twentieth-century Argentine writer, has experienced many long periods of insomnia. Although he rarely appears in his stories, he seems to have shared a part of the life of Ireneo Funes, the principal character of the short story "Funes the Memorious."

After being thrown by a horse, Ireneo becomes paralyzed and develops insomnia. He also acquires an uncanny ability to remember everything he reads, and he never forgets anything either. During his nightly vigils, he is forced to weave intricate labyrinths of data and store them like a computer. However, most of the stored information is useless, since he cannot sort it out and put it to practical use. With little effort he learns four languages, but he has few opportunities to put them into practice before his death two years later.

WRITING EXERCISE

Your fairly normal life has just been shattered by a paralyzing accident. You have movement only in the upper portion of your body. How would your life change? What would be your reaction to this drastic turn of events? How would you spend the time left in your life? Would you be able to adjust emotionally? Write an essay in which you react to this situation.

VOCABULARY EXPANSION

insomnia – unable to sleep

rarely – not very often, seldom

acquires – gets, obtains

uncanny – strange, mysterious

vigils – night watches

labyrinth – a maze

shattered – broken, greatly altered

paralyzed – physically unable to move due to muscle damage

weave – connect together different elements

intricate – complicated

WRITING EXERCISE

Here are additional essay topics to consider. How would you react to these situations?

- A thoughtless newspaper journalist has written an article in which he describes an unpleasant experience he had in your country during his recent trip there. He condemns all the people there as rude and unfriendly. He complains that all of the policemen are crooked because one gave him a ticket for speeding. Because he ate something that did not agree with him, he claims that the restaurants only want American dollars and serve tourists rotten food. Write a letter indicating how mistaken he is in his ideas. Tell the people how truly wonderful your country is and why they should visit there.

- In a nearby town the people have a volunteer fire department because the town cannot support a full-time crew. Each citizen is asked to pay a small amount of money to help maintain the equipment and the firehouse. Several of the wealthier people of the town refuse to pay because they feel that such a service is not needed. One night one of their houses catches fire and the firefighters do not respond to the call. Within forty-five minutes the house is completely destroyed. Write your reaction in a letter to the editor.

- A foreign snake handler has come to your community from another country, hoping to break a record set in the *Guinness Book of World Records*. He plans to spend 100 days in a specially designed tank with 24 deadly poisonous snakes. He assures everyone that nothing will happen, but the local emergency medical team, which works out of a building one block away, will be on the alert in the event that the man is bitten. Your tax dollars are going to pay for the emergency response that may occur due to this foolish and dangerous undertaking. How would you react to such a situation?

- Your checkbook balance shows that you have more money than your monthly bank statement. You receive a notice of four overdrafts of insufficient funds for which the bank withdraws an additional $100 from your account. Your credit rating and reputation are at stake. How will you attempt to rectify this error possibly on your part?

Other Topics for a Reaction Paper

- Your reaction to an unpleasant personal experience or that of a friend

- You have just won a $20 million lottery

- Flag burning

- Nude sunbathers on public beaches

- People who disobey no-smoking signs

- Someone has just written a very negative and untrue article about your country

- Someone with a criminal record has been elected to a government position in your city

- Your university will be closing its doors forever next month, and you have only one more semester until graduation.

ESSAYS ON STANDARDIZED EXAMS

Keep in mind that for an essay exam you will be provided with only one topic on which you can write. Look at the topics and imagine that each one represents a different exam. Develop as many of them as you can for practice.

Directions: You will have 45 minutes to develop this topic into a 250-word essay. There is ONE and ONLY ONE topic for this assignment. Develop it as best as you can recall, following the steps listed below:

- Think about the topic before you write.

- Make sure that you understand the topic.

- Brainstorm first, to get all your ideas together.

- Write a short outline so that you can plan your writing in a logical manner.

- Allow yourself enough time to proof your writing.

- Check for spelling, grammar, punctuation, and understanding.

- Revise your essay.

Topics for Writing Practice

Reaction

1. Your local newspaper has just featured a story about an 82-year-old woman who was sentenced to five years in prison for growing marijuana for her own

medical purposes. She is too poor to buy the medicine that she needs and has resorted to using marijuana because it alleviates the severe joint pain she has been suffering. You feel compelled to write a letter to the editor. How would you react to this seemingly unjust situation?

2. You live in a very peaceful upscale community, and the local government has decided to build an amusement park down the street. The traffic will be horrendous, the noise unbearable, and the park will destroy the natural beauty of your neighborhood. Write your reaction.

3. Abortion is a hotly debated topic, especially the type that favors partial-birth termination of pregnancy. This entails inducing the birth and then piercing the neck of the baby before it has completely left the birth canal. What is your reaction to this procedure?

4. You decide to join a group of friends for dinner at a very elegant restaurant. Your friends are non-smokers. You are a smoker. Before dinner you decide to light up at the table, but the hostess informs you that there is no smoking permitted anywhere in that restaurant. How would you react?

5. The governor of your state has decided to cut drastically education and financial aid to students. If you do not receive economic assistance, you will not be able to finish your studies and realize your dreams of becoming a doctor. Write a letter to the governor expressing your reaction to this plan.

6. Many people watched with great indignation as the Olympic judges awarded the gold medals in pair figure skating to the Russian couple instead of to the more deserving Canadians. Many feel that it was politically motivated. How do you feel about politics' playing a role in sports programs?

Process

7. Your family is planning a trip out West this summer. Describe your step-by-step preparation for this trip.

8. You are planning to have your own summer vegetable garden this year. What steps will you take to make your garden a reality?

9. You have an opportunity to participate in the Rose Bowl festivities on New Year's Day. Describe the process you will use to raise the money to make the trip.

10. All of us need to make every effort to control pollution in this country. Discuss your personal plan for preserving the planet.

11. Discuss the process you went through to apply to study in the United States.

12. Discuss the process for successfully acquiring a second language.

Description

13. Many authors have written about a utopian society. One of the elements of such a society would mean that people would become ageless. What would life be like in a society where no one ever grew older?

14. All of us at one time or another have had an embarrassing moment. Describe yours and tell how you reacted to it.

15. Success means different things to different people. Describe what success means to you and how you measure success in others.

16. Describe your hometown, country, or culture.

Comparison/contrast

17. Community colleges, an invention of the 1950s and 1960s, have been beneficial for students who have not yet decided on a career or for those desiring technical training only. How do community colleges differ from four-year colleges and universities? Why would you choose one over the other?

18. Students who live away from home while attending classes face the problem of housing accommodations. Some live in dormitories; others prefer living alone in apartments; while still others prefer living with a family. Explain which you prefer.

19. Young married couples today face the problem of deciding whether to buy a house or to rent an apartment. If you were faced with this dilemma, what would you choose to do?

20. Credit cards have been to many a salvation and to others an absolute disaster. How do credit cards affect your life? Discuss some of the advantages and disadvantages of having them.

21. Compare your hometown with the city where you are studying.

Persuasion

22. Many arguments on local and federal government levels revolve around the question of gun control. Many feel such legislation would be useless and that many crimes would still be committed. Should gun control laws exist and be strictly enforced?

23. Many countries are building nuclear weapons with the potential of annihilating the world's population. Should nations around the world be forced to abandon this policy and try to promote peace?

24. Many horrible crimes are committed in this country and the innocent victims sometimes suffer most. Some states provide compensation to the victims. Explain why you feel that these innocent people should (not) be compensated.

25. In American universities students maintain a broad area of study, while in foreign universities, a student's education focuses only on the studies in their area of specialization. Should a student study only within his area, or should he take courses in many different disciplines?

26. There is growing concern for highway safety in the United States. The government has suggested a law that would incarcerate anyone not using seat belts. Write a letter to your congressman expressing your view on this subject.

27. Should gambling be limited or banned in the city or state where you live?

28. Write an essay in which you try to persuade high school students in your country about the benefits of studying abroad.

Narrative

29. All of us at one time or another would like to change events in our past. If you could relive your high school years, what would you do differently?

30. The mayor in your town has asked you to write a tribute to the heroes of the terrorist attacks of September 11, 2001. What would you say in memory of these wonderful people?

31. Many people believe that a college education is necessary to find a good job. Discuss the advantages and disadvantages of completing a four-year, full-time program to get a good job.

32. Many people play the lottery every week, hoping to change their lifestyles and live a life of leisure. How would your life change if you won over $1 million?

Suggested Journal Topics

A Beautiful City	Winning the Lottery
A Memorable Occasion	Cars
An Interesting Person	Transportation
An Embarrassing Moment	Driving a Car
A Famous Person I Would Like to Meet	City Life versus Country Life
My Hometown	Campus Activities
Leisure Activities	Sewing
Sports	Painting and Drawing
Hobbies	Swimming (or other sports)
Weekend Activities	Seasons
A Trip to a Museum	Cooking
A Walk in the Park	Musicians
Preparing a Favorite Food	My Hero
Music	Sibling Rivalry
Dances	Schools in My Country
The Ideal Man/Woman	My Best Friend
Education	Shopping

Pets

Vacations

First Day in a New Town

A Stupid Law

Different Customs

Tests

Games

The Movies—Actors and Actresses

Typhoons/Monsoons

Learning a Foreign Language

Freedom

Doing the Laundry

The Cafeteria

Respecting the Rights of Others

Moving

Arriving on Time

Registering for Classes

Teachers (students)

College Life

Children

Hurricanes/Tornadoes

Graduation

Peace

Libraries

Language Labs

ESL
GLOSSARY

Glossary

ACTIVE VOICE – sentence structure in which the subject is responsible for performing the action of the verb. In the passive voice, the subject receives the action.

> The batter *hit* the ball.   The ball *was hit* by the batter.

ADJECTIVE – word that describes a noun or pronoun.

> red   round   excited

ADVERB – word that modifies a verb, adjective, or another adverb.

> quickly   fast   very

AGREEMENT – how words correspond to other words in a sentence or phrase.

> *Everyone* must pay *his/her* expenses before we leave for Rome.

CAPITALIZATION – writing words with a large or capital letter; refer to the section on capitalization.

CLAUSE – part of a sentence; main clauses (independent) can stand alone and convey a complete thought. Dependent (subordinate) clauses do not convey a complete idea even though they may contain a subject and verb. The latter need the main clause to give the whole structure meaning.

> *Because it was raining*, we had to cancel the picnic.

COLON – punctuation mark indicated by the symbol (:). Used to indicate that a series will follow.

> The following people attended the meeting: Tom, Harry, Sue, and Ellen.

COMMA – punctuation mark indicated by the symbol (,). Used to separate elements in a series, to separate complete sentences introduced by *and*, *but*, and so on.

COMMA SPLICE – two complete sentences joined by a comma

Tom got a raise, he bought a car.

DANGLING PARTICIPLE – participial phrase (V + ING or V + ED) at the beginning of a sentence that is not the subject and does not modify the noun or pronoun following the phrase.

Pounding the nail, the picture was finally hung.

DIRECT SPEECH – the exact words of someone, usually written between quotation marks.

Tom said, "I will attend the meeting at 8:00 tonight."

EMBEDDED QUESTION – one found within a sentence; follows pattern of Question Word + Subject + Verb.

I'm not sure when Ariel will arrive.

EXCLAMATION POINT – punctuation mark indicated by the symbol (!). Used to express elements of surprise.

Sharks! Get out of the water!

FRAGMENT – part of a sentence that does not convey a complete idea.

That morning in the park

GERUND – verb form ending in *-ing* that may be used as a noun.

Running is good exercise.

MAIN CLAUSE – in a sentence composed of two clauses, the main clause is the one conveying a complete thought.

Ellen took a vacation after she had finished the project.

PARALLEL STRUCTURE – keeping elements of a series all the same (all nouns, verbs, adjectives, adverbs, and so on)

Jogging, swimming, and dancing are good exercises.

PARTICIPLE – form of verb usually ending in ED (past) or ING (present)

frightened - frightening   fried - frying

PASSIVE VOICE – sentence structure in which the subject does not perform the action, but rather receives it; BE + past participle.

The play *was written* by Shakespeare.

PERIOD – punctuation mark using the symbol (.). Used mostly at the end of a sentence.

PREPOSITION – word relating a noun or pronoun to other words in a sentence (in, into, on, to, by).

The tickets are for the afternoon performance.

QUESTION MARK – punctuation mark using the symbol (?). Used after an interrogative statement, one in which the speaker asks for certain information.

When is your friend arriving?

QUOTATION – using someone's exact words.

Jane said, "*I will attend the meeting on Thursday.*"

RELATIVE PRONOUNS – ones that relate to the word that precedes them. These pronouns introduce a dependent clause (who, whom, that, which).

I know Dane Cameron, *who* is the director of Acme Computers.

RUN-ONS – two complete sentences joined without any punctuation.

It rained very hard we got wet and had an accident.

SEMICOLON – punctuation mark indicated by the symbol (;). Used when connecting related main clauses in a series or else when separating unlike entities of a series.

It rained very hard yesterday; therefore, we canceled the picnic.

SENTENCE – group of words containing a subject, a verb, and a complete thought.

Mrs. Davis drove to Chicago on Monday.

SEQUENCE OF TENSES – relationship in time of verbs used in a sentence.

The teacher *said* that we *would have* an exam on Friday.

SHIFT – unnecessary change from one grammatical element to another in a sentence or a paragraph.

> *Every* student needs a textbook to complete *their* lesson. (their = his/her)

SLANG – certain vocabulary unacceptable in formal writing.

> *kids* = children   *lousy* = awful

SUBORDINATE (DEPENDENT) CLAUSE – one that contains a subject and a verb, but one that does not convey a complete thought. It depends on the main clause to give it meaning.

> *Because it was raining very hard*, we were forced to cancel the bicycle races.

THESIS STATEMENT – sets the theme for the whole essay; lets readers know what type of paper it will be and what ideas the writer will develop.

TOPIC SENTENCE – the controlling idea of a paragraph; it relates to the thesis statement as one of the elements that the writer will develop in the paper.

TRANSITION – in writing, the change from one idea to another.

> Henry sent his post cards *after* he had returned from Europe.

TRANSITION WORDS – words used in writing to connect smoothly from sentence to sentence, paragraph to paragraph, or idea to idea.

> The show had already started, *but* we decided to go anyway.

VOICE – form of verb that shows whether the subject performs the action (active) or receives the action (passive).

> Vince *wrote* the poem in 1980. (active voice)

> The poem *was written* in 1980. (passive voice)

ESL
ANSWER KEYS

ANSWER KEYS

EXERCISE 1

1. simple	3. simple	5. simple	7. simple	9. compound
2. simple	4. compound	6. compound	8. compound	10. compound

EXERCISE 2:

1. F	3. F	5. C	7. F	9. C
2. F	4. C	6. F	8. F	10. F

EXERCISE 3:

1. C	5. C	9. C	13. F	17. C
2. C	6. F	10. C	14. F	18. C
3. C	7. F	11. F	15. C	19. F
4. C	8. F	12. F	16. F	20. F

EXERCISE 4:

what you have been doing lately
what topic I had finally chosen
what you are going to write
when you don't know
what you want to do
where they are sending him

what they will do about getting a house
how much they want for it
how much it is worth
when she got married
who the lucky guy is
when we can get together

EXERCISE 5:

1. whose books these are
2. where they were going
3. how many people will be attending
4. whom David called
5. which of the dresses Jane prefers?
6. where he comes from
7. how many cities they visited.
8. how old the twins are?
9. what time they left for school
10. how the microwave works
11. what happened to her car
12. what courses his sisters are studying
13. what "au revoir" means in English
14. what your mother bought at the supermarket
15. which car is Jerry's
16. when the plane from New York will arrive
17. why you missed class yesterday
18. how many letters she wrote to Beverly
19. what the lecture was about
20. how many stamps I need for this package

EXERCISE 6:

1. isn't he	6. weren't there	11. didn't he	16. doesn't it
2. does she	7. didn't they	12. won't they	17. haven't they
3. don't they	8. can't you	13. didn't they	18. did you
4. wasn't it	9. shouldn't he	14. didn't they	19. don't they
5. aren't they	10. don't they	15. doesn't he	20. won't there

EXERCISE 7:

1. After the movie, to the soda shop, for ice cream
2. from your uncle
3. until 4:30
4. among her children and their friends
5. in her elegant dress, at the top, of the spiral staircase
6. in our office, since 1985
7. during spring recess, to the beach
8. in this report
9. in the middle, of the afternoon
10. about who would, to the ball game
11. for them
12. in front of the library
13. behind the picture
14. over the mountains
15. at the bottom, of the lake
16. off the roof
17. between the refrigerator and the wall
18. for the car
19. under the circumstances
20. across the street

EXERCISE 8:

into a new house,
out of the boxes,
in the house,
in their proper places,
under cartons,
above the cupboards,
of days,
between one thing and another,
under plastic covers,
down the steps,
in the corner,
during the move
behind the furniture,
for a number,
through their things,
after the move

EXERCISE 9:

1. decided to go	9. prepared	17. safely
2. stood	10. left	18. difficult
3. to get	11. cried	19. We/My family
4. passport	12. stayed	20. customs
5. interviewed	13. English	21. live
6. sat	14. left	22. worry
7. asked	15. flew	23. happy
8. signed	16. plane	

EXERCISE 10:

1. Having already passed the street
2. finishing the project early.
3. While skiing in the mountains
4. Watching television non-stop for six hours
5. Seeing the terrible accident
6. Upon arriving at the pier
7. afraid of my seeing her with my boyfriend
8. Hovering over the airport
9. water skiing without a life jacket
10. Mona's taking so much medicine

EXERCISE 11:

1. E   Building an office complex in this area would create a problem for local residents.
2. G   Drinking and driving don't mix.
3. C   Swimming the English Channel as quickly as she could, Florence Chadwick broke the record. (Florence Chadwick broke the record, swimming the English Channel as fast as she could.)
4. I   Hiding in the cellar, the young girl escaped the soldier's search. (The young girl escaped the soldier's search BY hiding in the cellar.)
5. H   Shutting the window at night makes it quieter inside.
6. K   Flying through the air with the greatest of ease, the acrobats performed their stunts. (The acrobats performed their stunts, flying through the air with the greatest of ease.)
7. B   We listened to the wind blowing fiercely outside.
8. J   Sitting uneasily in her boss' office, the secretary waited for him to dictate the letters.
9. F   Wearing a ski cap in July, Ryan looked ridiculous. (Ryan looked ridiculous wearing a ski cap in July.)
10. D   Hitting the ball near the end of the bat will provide more distance.
11. M   Falling from the tree, Phil broke his arm in three places. (Phil broke his arm in three places AFTER falling from the tree.)
12. A   Cutting along the edge of the pattern allows for a $\frac{5}{8}$" seam.
13. L   Making peach pies made my grandmother very happy.

EXERCISE 12:

1. E   Cheryl's dropping the casserole sent pieces of glass flying everywhere.
2. J   Repeatedly speaking in public will make you feel more at ease. (You will feel more at ease BY repeatedly speaking in public.)
3. H   Diving into the deep murky waters, the crew hoped to find the buried treasure. (The crew hoped to find the buried treasure BY diving into the deep murky waters.)
4. K   Teaching younger children is quite a challenge.
5. C   Washing the windows provided a clearer and more beautiful view.

6. L Sinking into the frigid water near the iceberg, the great luxury liner disappeared. (The great luxury liner disappeared, sinking into the frigid water near the iceberg.)

7. I Leaving the house in a great hurry, Tom forgot to lock the door. (Tom forgot to lock the door, leaving the house in a great hurry.)

8. D Seth's teacher was very much upset when she caught him writing in the new library book.

9. G Forgetting his lines in the play, the actor decided to ad lib.

10. B Cooking eggs thoroughly guards against food poisoning.

11. F After providing more background light, the photographer took a number of pictures. (The photographer took a number of pictures after providing more background light.)

12. A Jenny preferred to stay home at night, reading a good book or watching a movie.

EXERCISE 13: SIGNING UP FOR CLASSES

running from office to office
filling out all of those forms
answering all the questions

finding some of the sections already closed
hurrying to see my counselor after spending
four hours on campus registering for classes

EXERCISE 14:

1. I entered the store
2. I selected a number of items
3. I decided I couldn't afford some of them.
4. I found most of the items on my list
5. I selected some onions, potatoes, and carrots.
6. I headed for the checkout
7. I watched the cashier ring up the order.
8. I drove home
9. is quite an experience!

EXERCISE 15:

1. Whenever you have time
2. whichever sweater you like
3. before she moved away
4. As you walked out the door
5. since we do not have enough food for the party
6. who bought that house
7. If you get the information before Tuesday
8. Except for when he was ill
9. As soon as you hear the results
10. as if she is enjoying the play
11. Despite Bobby's constant criticism
12. Wherever you travel
13. When the lights went out
14. because the plane arrived late
15. Even though the deadline had passed
16. since he was seven years old
17. where I can find the art museum
18. whom you saw in the park
19. whose son is your student
20. if they took more precautions

EXERCISE 16:

1. even though	4. that	7. After	10. so that
2. Despite	5. until	8. When/Whenever	
3. Whenever/When	6. As far as	9. Because	

EXERCISE 17:

1. Before	7. After	13. who	19. Unless, Until	25. whose
2. After	8. That	14. if	20. so that	
3. Because /Since	9. As	15. Unless	21. Whichever	
4. Because/Since	10. whom	16. Unless/Until	22. as if	
5. That	11. As	17. Wherever	23. Although/Even though	
6. Before	12. If	18. While	24. Even though	

EXERCISE 18:

1. As Nazi Germany was invading France in 1940
2. While searching for a lost dog
3. When the beam from their flashlight reflected against the lighter background of the walls of the cave
4. that they saw
5. After anthropologists had conducted considerable research
6. Although the animal forms were perfectly proportioned
7. which had been preserved for thousands of years in the airtight, moistureless caves
8. that these paintings represented some of the greatest art treasures in all of France
9. after scientists had spent a great deal of time preserving the paintings
10. Despite the caveman's primitiveness,

EXERCISE 19:

1. adverb	3. adverb	5. adverb	7. adverb	9. adjective
2. adverb	4. adjective	6. adverb	8. noun	10. adverb

EXERCISE 20:

It was Friday and I was looking forward to the weekend to relax. Despite some gray clouds in the sky, I left my umbrella and raincoat at home. Because of a sudden thunderstorm, there was a bad accident on the road, and I arrived late for work. Consequently, my boss was angry and disappointed because I was not at the 8:30 meeting to give my report. When I put my report in the copy machine, nothing happened, so I tried again, and due to a malfunction, it shredded my report instead of printing it. Since the only other copy was at home, I told my boss that I would return home to get it and have it on his desk in time to submit it to the committee. I had no umbrella and consequently got wet moving as fast as I could to my car in the parking lot. I decided to change clothes when I returned home. Then as I was hurrying, I bumped the corner of the coffee table and got a run in my stockings. Because my report arrived late, the committee postponed its decision on the project. So another Friday the 13th had passed, and I became one of its victims of bad luck. I decided to go home and try to forget everything that happened, including the shredded report.

EXERCISE 21:

The continent of Africa has the richest variety of flora and fauna in the world. Because it is located in jungle areas, there are many kinds of vegetation. These plants that surround the oases of the deserts are very beautiful. This continent can claim the diversity of fauna that breeds and roams the jungle areas. Many kinds of (species) of birds and snakes fly and slither throughout the area. Camels, lions, giraffes, elephants, gazelles, tigers, zebras, and antelopes are just a few of the wild animals that cross (roam) the grassy savannas every day. Besides the savannas, its physical geographic features include tropical rain forests, the Atlas Mountains, and the Sahara, Kalahari, and Namib Deserts. All of these natural phenomena provide shelter for a variety of species. Truly the continent of Africa provides the greatest diversity of flora and fauna in the world.

EXERCISE 22:

1. OK	8. OK	15. B	22. OK	29. B	36. B
2. B	9. OK	16. B	23. N	30. OK	37. B
3. B	10. B	17. B	24. B	31. OK	38. OK
4. B	11. B	18. OK	25. OK	32. N	39. B
5. OK	12. B	19. N	26. OK	33. OK	40. OK
6. B	13. B	20. B	27. OK	34. OK	
7. B	14. OK	21. B	28. OK	35. N	

EXERCISE 23:

1. B	4. A	7. A	10. B	13. B
2. A	5. B	8. B	11. B	14. A
3. A	6. A	9. A	12. B	15. A

EXERCISE 24:

1. B	4. A	7. A	10. A	13. B
2. B	5. A	8. B	11. B	14. B
3. A	6. B	9. A	12. B	15. B

EXERCISE 25:

1. verbs
2. verbs
3. verbs
4. nouns
5. nouns
6. gerunds
7. verbs
8. adj. + nouns
9. commands
10. gerunds
11. preposition
12. adjectives
13. gerunds
14. prepositions
15. verbs
16. verbs
17. adjectives
18. infinities

EXERCISE 26:

1. B in the safe, in the drawer
2. B barked, howled, ran
3. A hungry, tired, sick
4. B banker, property manager, salesman
5. A charismatic, handsome, conceited
6. A clawing the furniture, teasing the bird, playing with catnip
7. A along the beach, among the sea gulls, above the pebbles
8. B dresses, dances opera
9. B lighter colored, heavier, more expensive
10. B attractive, young, well-known
11. B music, sports, math
12. A dancing, drinking, smoking
13. A sick, underweight, hungry
14. B tripped, fell, sprained
15. A painters, sculptors, photographers
16. B run, swim, jog
17. B full, healthy, green
18. A examined the patient, gave a diagnosis, wrote a bill
19. B jump, run, ski
20. B homes, cars, race horses

EXERCISE 27:

1. B   2. B   3. A   4. A   5. B   6. B   7. B   8. A   9. B   10. B

EXERCISE 28:

1. B   2. B   3. B   4. A   5. A   6. B   7. B   8. A   9. B   10. A

EXERCISE 29:

1. A   2. B   3. B   4. B   5. A   6. A   7. B   8. B   9. B   10. A

EXERCISE 30:

1. A   2. B   3. A   4. A   5. B   6. B   7. B   8. B   9. B   10. A

EXERCISE 31:

1. B   2. B   3. B   4. B   5. B   6. B   7. A   8. A   9. B   10. B

EXERCISE 32:

1. B	5. C	9. A	13. B	17. C
2. B	6. B	10. B	14. B	18. C
3. A	7. C	11. A	15. B	19. A
4. A	8. C	12. B	16. A	20. C

EXERCISE 33:

1. RO	5. RO	9. RO	13. RO	17. CS
2. RO	6. RO	10. CS	14. CS	18. CS
3. CS	7. CS	11. CS	15. CS	19. RO
4. RO	8. RO	12. RO	16. CS	20. CS

EXERCISE 34:

1. CS	5. RO	9. RO	13. RO	17. CS
2. RO	6. CS	10. CS	14. RO	18. CS
3. CS	7. CS	11. RO	15. RO	19. RO
4. RO	8. CS	12. RO	16. RO	20. RO

EXERCISE 35: (POSSIBLE ANSWERS)

1. My sister is studying chemistry because she hopes to become a famous scientist.
2. The windows of the cottage were dark. Where was the rest of the family?
3. We rode until nearly dark, and then we raced home to supper.
4. He is an excellent dentist; he has a large office downtown.
5. Much depends upon your help. You won't fail us, will you?
6. We planned the design and carried it out on the leather. This took real skill.
7. Our parents went to New York to visit relatives.

8. All materials are similar in certain ways although they may not look or feel alike.
9. Electric current is not a material because it does not take up space.
10. There are three states of matter. Material is another name for matter.
11. He rested for two hours and then felt better.
12. The children ran into the street heedlessly. They never stopped to look either way.
13. The committee decided to hold a dance, and there would be an admission charge of one dollar.
14. The canoe plunged through the dangerous rapids as (while) water splashed the occupants.
15. I have fallen on my new skis many times, but I keep trying.
16. Let's have lamb chops since I'm tired of roast beef.
17. He attended high school in Denver, and then his family moved to Seattle.
18. Do you think it will rain and spoil our fun?
19. Please go to bed because it is getting late.
20. The trees were bare of leaves. How could it be summer?

EXERCISE 36:

1. B   2. B   3. B.   4. B   5. B   6. B   7. A   8. A   9. B   10. A

EXERCISE 37:

1. A	5. A	9. B	13. B
2. B	6. A	10. A	14. B
3. A and B	7. B	11. A	15. A
4. B	8. A	12. A	

CHAPTER REVIEW EXERCISE

1. A	5. A	9. C	13. B
2. A	6. C	10. C	14. A
3. C	7. C	11. C	15. B
4. C	8. A	12. C	16. B

EXERCISE 38:

1. 1&2	3. 3	5. 1&2	7. 1&2	9. 1&2
2. 3&5	4. 1&2	6. 3,4,5	8. 1&2	10. 3&5

EXERCISE 39:

1. OK young people
2. OK foreigners
3. OK those planning to marry
4. OK travelers, explorers
5. OK taxpayers, voters
6. incomplete, readers
7. incomplete, people getting insurance, salesmen
8. incomplete, Francesca
9. OK entertainers, viewers, promoters
10. incomplete, future parents, adoption agencies
11. OK EPA, citizens, environmentalists
12. OK students, faculty, administrators
13. OK if the writer can prove it.
14. OK couples planning marriage,
15. OK taxpayers, voters, Congress
16. incomplete, home owners
17. OK job seekers, employers
18. incomplete, students, teachers
19. incomplete, students
20. OK florists, home decorators

EXERCISE 40:

1. persuasion, reaction
2. narrative, persuasion
3. process
4. process
5. narrative, persuasion, comparison/ contrast
6. process, persuasion
7. process
8. Narrative, persuasion
9. Narrative, description, persuasion
10. Narrative, description, reaction, persuasion
11. Description, comparison/contrast
12. Narrative, description

EXERCISE 41: ANSWERS WILL VARY; SOME POSSIBILITIES:

Problems with technology have caused me several headaches lately.

It's obvious that Joseph Anderson has a talent for writing.

Although Leslie is studying medicine, she has encountered several difficulties in the past week.

EXERCISE 42: ANSWERS WILL VARY; SOME POSSIBILITIES:

*The number of violent acts in a one-hour show has increased.

*Children's emotional needs are not met.

*The plan calls for an increase in salaries as well as in class size.

*De-icing planes causes considerable delays in take-off and landing.

*Students who do not do well all semester won't improve on their final exam.

EXERCISE 43: HALLOWEEN

1. The author will discuss how the celebration of Halloween has changed over the centuries.
2. The religious aspects of Halloween
3. They all point to the religious aspects of Halloween.
4. Yes.
5. The conclusion summarizes the whole essay and the religious aspects.
6. Yes.
7. Yes. Readers know that the author has nothing more to say.

EXERCISE 44: FALLINGWATER

1. along, in the distance, above, among, over, over, below, on all sides, across the stream, surrounding, to the left
2. in spatial order
3. yes, they all describe how Fallingwater is a great architectural masterpiece

EXERCISE 45: THE PISAQ RUINS

and, suddenly, Before, As soon as, Immediately, Soon after, In a few moments, afterwards, and, after that, Suddenly, in front of, but, certainly, finally, and, previously, on the contrary, Gradually, However, at last, once, and, and, in a short time, later, and.

EXERCISE 46: WAYNE

1= adds information   2= part of a process
3= shows contrast   4= draws a conclusion

Besides = 1	and = 1	Next = 2
Nevertheless = 3	however = 3	finally = 2
Rather than = 3	also = 1	Consequently = 4
Consequently = 4	so = 2	Furthermore = 1
Therefore = 4	however = 3	Therefore = 2
also = 1	and = 1	otherwise = 3
Otherwise = 3	Instead = 3	otherwise = 3
	and = 1	and = 1

EXERCISE 47: SOLAR ECLIPSE

A solar eclipse occurs when the moon passes between the sun and the earth, and the three form a straight line. There is a large shadow on Earth causing some areas to be in darkness. Not all places see the same amount of the eclipse. The closer an area is to the total eclipse, the less light people are able to see. Although the moon appears to cover the sun completely, it is only an illusion. The moon is one four-hundredth as large as the sun, but the moon is closer to the earth and appears to block the sun out. The next total solar eclipse visible in North America will take place in the year 2017, some 38 years after its predecessor. Scientists advise those watching the eclipse not to look directly at the sun. To do so could damage the retina of the eye and cause irreversible blindness.

EXERCISE 48: YELLOWSTONE NATIONAL PARK

The state of Wyoming has many parks, but the most beautiful is Yellowstone National Park. Here, millions of acres provide a natural habitat for moose, bears, elk, and deer. They wander freely, grazing on the lush green grass and provide tourists with interesting scenes to photograph. A friend of ours asked me, "What was the most exciting thing you saw there?" I replied, "The fascinating geyser, Old Faithful." There are many geysers, mud holes, and hot springs, but Old Faithful is the biggest and most spectacular. My friend asked, "Can anyone visit there most of the year?" I told my friend that people visited here all year except when the snow is very high in winter. Recently, they have had many forest fires there and tourists could not enter. It's too bad that careless smokers destroy the environment that we foreigners would like to enjoy on our visits.

EXERCISE 49: ESCAPE

1. This title is an attention getter.
2. Escape leads me to think of a release from a terrible situation.
3. First sentence about rifle-toting police inspires fear.
4. She wasn't carrying a certain letter. Fear of luggage search, delays and missing the plane, fear of being caught, agonizing wait, sweaty palms, shaking hands, walls closing in, going through Passport Control, the officer's hesitation, children were frightened
5. rifle-toting military police, detaining her and the children, demand a special letter, search luggage
6. The thesis statement, announcement about the flight delay, being caught, imprisoned, dark and damp cell, sweating palms, etc.
7. No, it seems very real
8. Yes
9. Trying to escape home problems, problems with the police, yearning to be free
10. answers will vary

NOTES

NOTES

NOTES

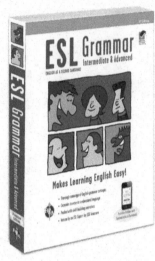

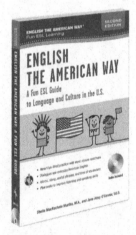
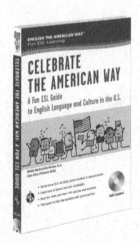